Fra Angelico

THIS VOLUME, EDITED BY ANDRE GLOECKNER,
WAS FIRST PUBLISHED IN JUNE MCMXLIX
BY THE HYPERION PRESS.   COLOUR BLOCKS
ENGRAVED BY CLICHES UNION AND REH,
PHOTOGRAVURE ENGRAVED
AND PRINTED BY IMPRIMERIE SAPHO,
TEXT BY ARTRA, COLOUR PLATES PRINTED
BY IMPRIMERIE MERSCH, PARIS.

Fra Angelico

BY

GERMAIN BAZIN

CURATOR AT THE MUSEUM OF THE LOUVRE
PROFESSOR AT THE ECOLE DU LOUVRE

TRANSLATED FROM THE FRENCH
BY
MARC LOGÉ

THE HYPERION PRESS

LONDON - PARIS - NEW YORK

FOREWORD

Perilous is the situation of the critic who tackles as popular a subject as Fra Angelico. He finds himself faced with a body of ideas and images whose temptation he must endure. He must wade through all the literary and critical sediments deposited by forerunners in order to rediscover the work in its original nude purity. But while escaping from the principle of authority, does he not run the risk of yielding to an artificial desire of originality?

There must be some mystery in Fra Angelico, fascinating to some, irritating ot others, as few artists have given rise to as considerable a quantity of studies. The numerous authors who have taken an interest in his work fall into two groups. For some, who are Catholic writers, the mystery of Fra Angelico is a Christian mystery. The radiance of his work is none other than that of his sainthood; favoured with supernatural graces, he made his talent serve the expression of his visions. His work must therefore, like the great masterpieces of mystical literature, be considered as a revelation of the beyond; such was even then the opinion of Vasari, the old biographer of the Italian Masters. Art historians who have studied Fra Angelico have sometimes affected to despise the pious writers. In his monumental history of Italian painting, which was so unfortunately interrupted by death, the late lamented Raymond Van Marle speaks with disdain of this " sentimental and unhealthy literature. " This is being harsh indeed and still more unfair. While certain works of theologico-mystical colour do not rise above the level of the usual edifying literature demanded by the faithful, the works of Father Beissel, of Strunk and Henri Cochin have permitted to define the position of Fra Angelico with respect to the great religious currents of his time.

The plastic interpretation of the painter's work and his position with respect to the Renaissance, which do not interest pious writers, are on the contrary points on which the attention of art historians is brought to bear. The latter are divided by a great debate : Does Fra Angelico belong to the Middle Ages or to the Renaissance?

Langton Douglas, Supino, Muratoff, are of latter opinion; the former, upheld by Miss Frida Schott-muller, is backed by the high authority of Bernard Berenson. Adopting an intermediate position, Van Marle sees in Fra Giovanni the most characteristic painter of the transition between the Gothic and the Renaissance.

The gentle figure of the angelic brother has thus provoked a quarrel between clerics and laymen and a controversy between art historians. We shall try in this book to keep as far from the one as from the other. And indeed the matter of knowing whether Fra Angelico belongs to the Middle-Ages or the Renaissance has no longer the same interest for us. Having to prospect the immense field of the past, the xixth century historians divided it up into sections, raising a wall around each of these, in order to enable each one to work quietly in his own field. The task on which our contemporaries are bent is that of breaking down these barriers, which limit the horizon, and to seek, beyond categories defined by intelligence, the continuity of historical evolution.

THE CHRISTIAN HUMANIST

IN the margin of his remarkable work on Piero della Francesca, Mr. Roberto Longhi has noted a very precious indication as to the evolution of Florentine art in the xvth century. He distinguishes, parallel with the innovatory line of which Donatello and Masaccio are the leaders, what he terms the " elegant mediaeval classicism " of which Ghiberti is the most representative figure. Struck by this idea, Mr. Muratoff extends it very happily to a whole group of artists of the first half of the Quattrocento : Fra Angelico, Masolino, Michelozzo, Luca della Robbia. For him Ghiberti is Fra Angelico's true emancipator. To be sure, these two artists are related by a similar love of harmony; however, Mr. Muratoff, inspiring himself more or less from the thesis of Mr. Bernard Berenson, considers this grouping as a traditional, — nay even backward — medium, foreign to the really creative movement of the Quattrocento. A mistaken theory. The mind refuses to consider as retrograde a tendency which terminates in Raphael. Will not the latter give a definitive form to the old dreams of classicism which had been haunting the Italian soul since two centuries ? This classical current is indeed one of the most authentic expressions not only of Italian but also of Western art. It traverses the desperate lyricism of the Middle-Ages through and through, and though time and again submerged under the baroque vegetation, it reappears periodically, infrangible.

The history of western thought is animated by a long debate on the meaning of the universal. Mediterranean peoples perceive the universal through the general, whereas Nordics do so through the multiple. The ones, thanks to a processus of increasing abstraction, tend to include the plurality of the world within a few concepts and to reduce the Whole to the One, whilst the others in the living multiplicity of its infinite changeableness, seek to seize the universe. A simple vision of things would show us the Middle Ages under the domination of the second of these principles, and the triumph of the former in the classical culture elaborated by the Renaissance. In reality, these constants deeply impressed the development of all Western civilization. The ardent lyricism of the Middle Ages must not make us forget how greatly that period was attracted by the classical sense of the universal. The concept of the Universals is a resurgence of Platonic archetypes, and scholastic philosophy has elaborated an orderly universe as harmonious and neat as a beautiful classical garden from which all mystery is banished. This is perhaps one of the grandest attempts man has ever dared to make to project into the world the order which reigns in his mind.

Western mediaeval art is an illustration of this dispute. The prodromes of classicism appear in Carolingian art which strives to stem the ornamental amorphism of the Barbarians. Although

9

in architecture it created some of the finest classical rhythms, in sculpture romanesque art gives free course to the polymorphic genius of the North, and engenders a marvelous universe of forms which reverberate to the Infinite through successive metamorphoses. It would seem as if, at the Gothic period, an inversion in technique took place. In France in the XIIIth century architecture abandons itself with delight to the joy of abolishing all notion of limitation, whilst sculpture gives so perfect a definition of classicism that it is possible to compare it to that which Attica had created eighteen centuries earlier. To romanesque polymorphism Gothic genius strongly opposes that unitary spirit which includes the possible infinity of forms within the cadences and canons of harmony. To the multiple romanesque capital, succeeds the capital decorated with crockets which in the Gothic art of the XIIIth century, is as uniform as the Greek Doric capital of which it is indeed the last avatar. Nowhere is one as struck by the opposition of the two styles as at Vezelay. On leaving that prodigious nave where a world of forms swarming on the capitals offers one inexhaustible invitations to dream, the Gothic choir, with all its identical capitals, merely proposes to the imagination one unique direction, one number, and produces a curious impression of classic coldness. Eternal stumbling-block of a perfection which tends naturally to that invariableness from which academism proceeds !

Before taking her flight, Italy seems to have awaited the Gothic example. This alone will be able to undo the fetters which held her prisoner in the toils of Byzantinism, in spite of an attempt, which had no morrow, to resume direct contact with antique classicism (1). The Gothic order is a spring-board from which Giovanni Pisano and Giotto both take their *élan*. Nevertheless a tendency which will always secretly contradict this classic vocation, deeply embedded in the Italian soul, appears in them. It is a proud sense of the greatness of man and of his destiny which drives the ultramontane towards the expression of force and the affirmation of energy. All along a line which from Giovanni Pisano and Giotto leads to Michael Angelo, and which is marked out by such men as Masaccio, Jacopo della Quercia, Donatello, Piero della Francesca, Mantegna, this obsession of force contracts harmony and begets an expressionism foreign to that renouncement of the individual exacted by the laws of classicism. The birth of the true tradition of harmony should be sought for in Andrea Pisano who, renouncing the expressive violence of Giovanni Pisano, and the stern greatness of Giotto, draws directly from the sources of French classicism. Nothing resembles more closely the first door of the Baptistery of Florence than certain bas-reliefs of Notre-Dame of Paris. Andrea softens with Attic grace Giotto's Spartan line; he flexes it to oblige it to follow certain rhythmical balancings, and creates that flexible Mozartian cadence of which Raphael will give so many examples. At the same time as he seeks for a just and successful partitioning of space (the hexagonal bas-reliefs of the Dome campanile are remarkable from this point of view), he tempers the gesticulatory mimicry and the physionomical expression, and makes countenances irradiate that abstract calm which springs from the classic sentiment of the constancy of the creature in the becoming, which illumines the brows of the statues of the French XIIIth century. Andrea Pisano's initiative will be followed with greater severity by Andrea Orcagna, and with a more refined sense of elegance by Nino Pisano, his own son, as well as by the unknown author of the bas-reliefs of the Dome of Orvieto. Then Ghiberti becomes the depository of the tradition, and he admits his devotion to it in the second door of the Baptistery. In the same monument Luca della Robbia will profess the same veneration for the great ancestor. These works preserved from the competition instituted in 1401 for the second door of the Baptistery, represent perfectly the two tendencies which, at the dawn of the XVth century, confront each other in the Florentine school. The *Abraham and Isaac* by Ghiberti combine, in an harmonious balancing, the former his sacrificatory gesture, the latter his attitude as victim. The patriarch prepares himself to immolate Isaac with all the elegance of a ballet dancer, whilst in Brunelleschi's picture he throws himself with an aggressive violence upon the contracted body of the child, and with a poignant gesture which Rembrandt will reinvent, turns his son's head upwards in order to offer his throat to the sacrificatory knife.

---

(1) The attempt made by Frederic II in Apulia.

Donatello and Ghiberti are the sources of the two main currents which feed the Florentine art of the Quattrocento. In Donatello the true plastic tradition of Giovanni Pisano and of Giotto, — which will reach its apex in Michael Angelo, — is continued. He conceives form by means of volumes, and places the accent on the nodulous summits of the relief; drapery plays, as on the stage, the rôle of amplificator of forms and of expression. On the other hand Ghiberti revives the " gothico-classical " sense of the arabesque; drapery and modelling appear conceived in function of the line of which they provoke the flow, folds, resilience, and balancing, all generators of cadence. Ghiberti was long eclipsed by Donatello's gigantic shadow; his rôle in the formation of the Florentine Quattrocento is only just beginning to be revealed. Old histories of art consider him as isolated and some even as belated. To-day the antecedents and consequents are beginning to appear, and reveal him as one of the links of that harmonious tradition which ends in Raphael. For what is nearer to the Door of Paradise than the Chamber of the Signature ?

Fra Angelico is one of the fleurons of this fruitful tradition. Therefore far from being behind his times or a man of another age, he becomes essentially integrated into the living and innovating evolution of Italian art. He shares the plastic preoccupations of the painters of his time; like them he seeks the truth; but, far more than they, he makes beauty and harmony the end of his art. Whereas Masaccio imposes to space and to volumes a contraction and tension which impart to them an expressive violence, Fra Angelico creates between all the different elements of a picture a succession of eurythmic relations. Like Ucello or Castagno he conceives space as a closed, limited world like a body; but whilst others precipitate it into the whirl of perspective he rounds it off in an harmonious curve. A happy partitioning of surface and depth, the indispensable relation between the enveloped and the enveloping forms, some of Raphael's works alone communicate that impression of eurythmy which emanates from a work such as the *Annunciation* of the third cell in the Convent of S. Mark (pl. 120). In it space is so exactly proportioned to the human figure, that it appears an effect of its measures. This is the very essence of classicism; Poussin will later express it in landscape. The anatomical exactness of the bodies, and the expression of the gestures, are limited by laws which cadence imposes to them. A gesture will never exceed this norm in order to accentuate expression as in the case of Masaccio, but in return the cadence will never distort the truth. This just accord has only been reached by certain happy epochs, and more particularly by the vth century in Greece, and by the xiiith century in France. Raphael will transgress truth in favour of harmony, and in that sense he will perhaps be more of a classicist than a classic, and, with him, all the French of the xviith century. Let one consider attentively a figure such as the headsman of whom one has a back view, brandishing his sword, in the *Martyrdom of St. Cosmas and St. Damian*, in the Louvre (pl. 135). The élan of the body, its balance, its *détente* in the very act, are represented with remarkable exactness. And yet the constitution of that body with its concise volumes and the cadence of the gesture present a rhythmical ensemble. Let us examine in Masaccio's work a personage seized thus in the very accomplishment of a violent action, such as for example the Magdalen in the *Crucifixion* at Naples, or the *St. Peter* taking the piece of money out of the fish's mouth at the Brancacci Chapel, or again — if it is really his work — the headsman of the *Decapitation of St. Paul* at Berlin. Here the harmonic limitation of the gesture is enforced with a view to dramatization : as in the plays of Corneille and Racine. Nothing in the history of forms recalls as much that little figure in *The Martyrdom of St. Cosmas*, than the bas-reliefs of the months in French cathedrals of the xivth century in which the gestures of labour are represented with such exactness, both as to veracity and to harmony. Just as in the case of Fra Angelico's headsman, each seems the quintessence extracted from the sum total of all the individual gestures corresponding to that particular action, something like the limit towards which all the particular possibilities of a determined act tend : its archetype. Therein is contained, translated into forms, a principle that is related to the theory of the Universals who believed they could reach the ultimate reality of things through the genera and the species, but not through the individuals : through the universal, but not through the singular.

The Platonic atmosphere of the first Renaissance in which Fra Angelico lived, is noways in opposition to the contemplative reveries on the universal in which delighted the thought of the Middle-Ages, so enamoured with Plato through the intermediary of Plotinus. It proceeds from it on the contrary, and differs from it only by the concept of unity which, in the Middle-Ages, consists in God, the personification of the transcendentals, and which for the Platonists of the Renaissance, readers of the " Banquet ", terminates in " Beauty ", which " is alone in itself in the unity and eternity of its form, whilst all other things are beautiful by their participation in this Beauty. "

Michelozzo and Fra Angelico have best expressed, the one in architecture, the other in the art of painting, that strictly Medicean concept which turns Beauty into a philosophy and an ethics. Was not the goal of human life as Cosimo de Medici practised it, and as Marcilio Ficino taught it to attain that perfect harmony of being which is accord with itself? This unity of the whole being was the object of the pedagogy of the Quattrocento, and in particular of that dispensed by the famous noble college of Mantua, where Vittorio da Feltre fashioned the aristocratic consciences of his time. This intimate order must be realized by the equilibrium of all the faculties, the sensual as much as the spiritual; thus " the complexity of the soul is no longer a necessary discord... human destiny is no longer a conflict between desire and renouncement " (1). The notion of proportion and of measure finds itself transported even into human life which is conceived as a game composed of relations : the goal each man pursues is to make a " masterpiece " of his own life.

For Fra Angelico the contemplation and realization of Beauty is the supreme goal of life and of art. But as a Christian disciple of Plato, he places Beauty in a necessary relation to the Divinity of whom it is one of the attributes. Perhaps one should say that for the Neo-Platonists of the Renaissance the relation is reversed : the Divine becomes the attribute of the Beautiful. But, in these times of peace, there existed no profound antinomy between the Christian ideal of perfection and the philosophical ideal of wisdom. The import of the Renaissance has been rather warped by the notion of revolution and of conscious reaction against the Middle-Ages which Burckhardt has introduced. It is easy for the latter to invoke the satirical and anticlerical literature which flourished in Italy in the xivth century; this is more an expression of the Middle-Ages than of the Renaissance. Burckhardt sets no great store by the dreams of philosophical and Christian syncretism that animated such humanists as Pico della Mirandola and Marcilio Ficino. Even the Church itself indulged in them. In his book which is one of the most nuanced to have been written on Fra Angelico, Henry Cochin has sketched with great sensibility the picture of the Florentine and Ponti-fical intellectual society in the second quarter of the xvth century. He has shown the harmony which reigned at that time between humanism and religion, and how the Dominicans of the Florentine Convent contributed to it. The suave and gentle St. Antoninus, prior of the Convent of St. Mark, who, in a celebrated dispute, took the defense of Christian learning against that of the Ancients, was a very subtle humanist who quoted Ovid if need be ; he merely forbade the use of such quotations in sermons. The very interdiction proves that the preachers of the time did not fail to weave into the precepts of the Gospel those of the sages of Antiquity. Certain of the philosophers who used to frequent Cosimo's platonist academy were churchmen. The Popes themselves practised what they preached : those who called Fra Angelico to work at the Vatican were both pious humanists. Speaking of Nicholas V who dreamed to awaken the Eternal City from its torpor, Pastor can say that with him " the Christian Renaissance took possession of the Pontifical see. " In the second half of the century, this harmonious syncretism led up to the angelic figure of Pico della Mirandola who lived like a saint and thought like a theosophist.

The works of Fra Angelico are not wholly consecrated to the supernatural. The mystic did not paint saints and madonnas only; a careful examination reveals here and there some of the noble faces, illumined by the light of intelligence, which belonged to the humanists of his time. If he depicted some of the loftiest expressions of the soul, soaring free of corporeal ties towards the Divine, neither was he unaware of the serenity imparted to the gaze and brow by the poise of antique wisdom; sometimes in a single ensemble both ideals are set side by side. In the Studiolo of Nicholas V, it is truly a metaphysical élan which transfigures the emaciated traits of St. Bona-ventura (pl. 154) while the powerful features of the Pontiff judging St. Stephen, whose physionomic

---

(1) *Laurent le Magnifique* by MARCEL BRION.

type is similar, have the majesty of an antique philosopher. The Renaissance conceived an ideal of the Platonic sage whose model Leonardo da Vinci provides in his own features. Raphael, in the School of Athens, gives these lineaments to his Plato. A fine, bare countenance of an Olympian calm, divided with harmonious symmetry by the two flowing streams of beard, is it not strange that it should appear several times in the work of the *frate*, mingled with the faces of saints or else in the guise of some Roman magistrate? More than Masaccio who was haunted by Roman grandeur, did Fra Angelico have a prescience of the ideal of beauty which the Greeks embodied in the face of the adolescent; by a trait of genius, he rejoins Phidias at a time when his contemporaries, in their effort to rediscover the plastic art of the Ancients, did not go back further than the age of Augustus or the art of Alexandria.

This brotherly understanding was to be of short duration. Humanism was soon to slip towards paganism : Pius II was to inaugurate the pagan Popes of the Renaissance. But before the convulsionary awakening of the grim Savonarola, Florence was to know a rare moment of poise and peace. No doubt the most perfect expression of that humanism was the Convent of St. Mark. It deserves, like the Portico or the Academy, to give its name to a form of culture which reached its golden age in the Florence of the second quarter of the xvth century, and which one might well call the "Medicean culture". Everything in it was the creation of the Medici. This convent was the realization of one of Cosimo's thoughts. Not content with having founded it, re-edified it, and established in it that Dominican order which was venerated in his family, he assembled in it everything that captivated his mind. What a new meaning those immaterial frescoes by Fra Angelico assume if one remembers that not far from them, in the garden of the great cloister of St. Dominic, mutilated statues of Venus and of Apollo celebrated the beauty of the body ! Cosimo had assembled his collection of antiquities in this refuge of holy silence. On the first floor, Michelozzo had built a library with silvery arcades; there, the records of Christian learning and the exhumed traces of Pagan lore accumulated side by side on the shelves under the attentive care of the scholarly Thomas di Sarzano, who was later to become Pope Nicholas V. Not far from there Cosimo had his own cell which the best pupil of the *frate* had decorated with an *Adoration of the Magii*, a discreet homage rendered to the maecenas of the convent. One imagines " the father of his country " seeking rest from the world, and coming to spend a few hours in this convent which was like a sort of cultural dependency of his own palace... In some old Greek manuscript he discovers the thought of the Fathers and poets of antiquity, he gladdens his eyes with the carnal beauty of antique marbles lifts his soul to the spectacle of celestial beatitude before the frescoes of Fra Giovanni, then strolls slowly under the arcades of the cloister of St. Antoninus whilst pursuing in himself the harmonious blending of all his thoughts and sensations. Or else, retiring within himself in his own cell, he places this tribute of beauty at the feet of the Child whom the Magii adore. So much insistance has been laid after Burckhardt on the paganism of the Renaissance that one is tempted to imagine that with those maecenas and philosophers the religious sentiment was a mere social conformism. Yet it was sincere with them, but ceased to require exclusively all the faculties of the creature; it became a mode of elevation of the soul, a means of acceding to wisdom; faith became a part of the system of thoughts and sentiments the man of the first Renaissance lived by, as an indispensable element of culture with which he nourished his soul. The self-control and resistance to passions to which Christianity accustoms the believer, favoured this state of calm self-possession obtained by the will of a clear consciousness of every act, thought, and sentiment; and that is one of the most remarkable traits of the Mediterranean conception of life. The chief virtue presiding over the ethics of the Medicean man is that of temperance. An attentive sentinel, it watches in order to prevent all excess capable of introducing instability into the soul. And in order to ensure a permanence to the being throughout its successive states, it checks every excessive tendency of desire.

Rare are indeed in history those perfectly poised moments when man, committing the Faustian sin, says to the passing instant : " Delay a moment, thou art so perfect ! " The Tuscan civilization of the second quarter of the xvth century was one of those moments. The pilgrim through centuries seems to interrupt his fatal course, and having reached a summit halts in order to behold both slopes : he then perceives that the goal of life is not beyond him but within reach of his hand. One understands that Germanic thinkers such as Oswald Spengler (1) have pronounced anathema against the Florentine civilization accusing it of sterility. Furious with becoming, they are unaware of the greatness and elation of that possession of the being which is a victory of man over time. It alone can secure for the being that happiness towards which the latter naturally tends, and which withdraws each time it seems to be on the point of reaching it in the course of those successive " euphories " which the ardour of its desire determine. The Medicean man discovers bliss in that self-possession which opposes itself to the tension of the soul straining to escape from itself : it reaches this state by a supreme operation of the spirit which transforms each thought and sensation into a contemplative act, and suppresses passion as the motive power of human life.

The only phrase of Fra Angelico's which has been brought down to us through the intermediary of Vasari is quite true to this Medicean concept of life. " He was in the habit of saying that Art demands much composure ", writes the old biographer. This is an essential phrase in its very simplicity, and one which leads one to glimpse in Fra Giovanni a peaceful soul far removed from the ardent mystical states of the Middle-Ages. One knows nothing of the frate's intimate biography, but I am inclined to believe that he can not have been a visionary after the manner of St. Catherine of Siena, or of St. Francis of Assisi, and that his piety must have been much nearer to devotion than to ecstasy. I think one would be wrong in imagining the peaceful refuge of the Convent of St. Mark as having witnessed the passionate ardours of the angelic painter's soul projected outside of itself by the attraction of the supernatural. If he made of his painting an act of faith, it was for him a form of prayer, a " vital orison " rather than a visionary expression. He was also to say : " *In order to treat of the things of the Christ one must live with the Christ* ". Indeed Fra Angelico lived in a pious familiarity with the holy personages he used to depict, but this mystic company does not seem to have provoked in him that tension which causes the saints to live on a supernatural plane, and which manifests itself in their lives by ecstatic phenomena.

---

(1) *The Decline of the Occident*, by OSWALD SPENGLER.

THE MONK

F AR from being opposed to the Medicean contemplation of beauty the conventual atmosphere in which Fra Angelico lived was on the contrary favourable to it. By renouncing desire the regular finds in the monastery the certitude of a profound peace which shelters him from worldly vicissitudes and violences. The cloister is a perfect image of this state of stability. The circular deambulation it offers one suggests the contemplative evolution of a thought describing orbs around a center. It is the circular movement which Dante adopts in the Divine Comedy as the symbol of the gravitation of the soul around the light. The infinite thus finds itself circumscribed in an infinitesimal point : God. The universe is reduced to a concentric ensemble of dogmas, images, sensations, and rites. The whole of monastic life obeys this cyclical rhythm; it is a perpetual recommencement of acts, prayers, and thoughts; the individual soul is crushed between the millstones of prayer and of conventual exercices. Every two hours the monk is seized again and thrown back into the crucible of common life; the time left " free " by the psalmody of the Book of Hours, is devoted to intellectual or manual work, each day the Abbot distributes it according to an order determined by himself alone. At the refectory, the voice of each reader is condemned to assume the common vesture left by his predecessors. Thus all day long the monk escapes from himself. For him the real danger is at night, because then he finds himself once more abandoned to all the temptations of personal life. It is the awaiting of anguish-tinged night that we feel quivering in the Office of Complines. The Church grows suddenly dim; only a few faint lights continue to burn, so that the monk should already become accustomed to night; in the darkness a chant wavers like a breath. The choir abandons the monodic style of the psalmody, and adopts the virtue of melody in order to infuse more warmth into the imploration it casts towards God whom it begs to avert from it the perils of the shadows of night. Something like an echo of the ancestral terror of night thrills in the voice of the monk which assumes a truly nocturnal semitone accent :

> " Procul recedant somnia
> Et noctium phantasmata. "

Here cometh the dark with all its cortege of dreams, nightmares, and demons. It is the hour of the temptation of the flesh...

> " Ne polluantur corpora. "

It is the hour when memories crowd in upon the brother's heart, and when arises in him the temptation of the " ascedia ", — that aridity of the soul produced by mortification. Succeeding to humble supplication, the serene chant of the " Regina Coeli " mounts suddenly, glowing with trust and filial love. The monk's voice becomes tender, insinuating like that of the child he used to be, and who uttered the blessed name of his mother before adventuring into the unknown of night.

There is another critical moment in the unfolding of a man's day — i.e. that hazy quarter of an hour which precedes his rising. It is then that, in the case of insomniacs, that tornado of anguish which Jules Romains so justly calls " the squall of sunrise ", breaks loose upon the soul. All the foundations upon which our ego is built are shaken by it. But the effects of a peaceful and restoring slumber also contain some germs of unrest. At certain happy moments of organic youth, the soul resuscitating slowly from the lethargy of sleep, finds itself as if renewed at the dawn of day. It oscillates uncertainly, tempted by all the confused desires floating within it; deliciously lazy, it abandons itself to a nonchalant indetermination for that brief instant which precedes the one when it will don again the armour of acquired thoughts, sentiments, and gestures. Thus dawn breaks upon a new life; we recover that naive joy of youth which glimpses, shimmering before it, the mysterious light of an unknown existence, the potential strength of which it can feel beating in its heart. In the meanders of dream the day presents itself to us as an unknown experience; we have the feeling of being once again in a state of native disponibility, having our whole life before us to create. 'Tis a state of pure desire — the Christian moralists would say of " concupiscence " — ferment of all temptations. The monastic rules apply a radical remedy against the dangers produced by the fluctuations of the soul which has been overwhelmed in too deep a sleep, as against the temptation which follows in the wake of insomnia. In the middle of the night the bell begins to toll dragging the monk roughly from his couch, and casting him back once more, still bemused, into the collective mould. Thus divided into two halves by the Office of Matins, sleep loses that lethargic value which causes the soul to recover its inherent virtues, restoring it to its *habitus* whilst being delivered from those habits. Thus monastic discipline does not cease pursuing the individual even during the relaxation of sleep, which can be likened to the light dozing of the soldier who knows he must rise during the night to take his turn at mounting guard. Rest itself becomes a monastic exercise.

Slowly crushed and broken on the grindstone of the hours, time, reduced to dust, is abolished. The life of a monk has neither beginning nor ending. It revolves upon itself in a perpetual revolution, in the lithurgic round of " hours ", and of years which confers to all the ritual acts and prayers not only a commemorative value but an actual import. Thus the monk has the sentiment of living outside the historical succession of events, outside the " world ", in a sort of anticipation of that blissful eternity towards which his whole life tends. This precession of the future continually projects futurity into the present, abolishes the past, and suppresses time. In the light of contemporary science, time is a given dimension of the universe and which man perceives relatively by displacing himself in it just as, by moving through space, he creates its perspective and extent. The notion of the passing of time from which man derives the anguish of living must therefore efface itself in an ethics which abolishes from life the sense of tension, that is to say of direction, of progress through the fourth dimension, in order to substitute to it a perpetual gravitation around a point in which the thoughts, acts, and sentiments which determine a human life, are fixed once for all.

By limiting the scope of his life to a restricted space, the monk already places himself in those conditions favourable to the non-perception of time. Man measures progression in time by a displacement in space, and the successions in space by the passing of time; thus by limiting human life to circumscribed horizons, one is apt to obscure the chronological sense. It is to this end that tend all those modes of life localized in space, such as the life of the peasant, of the bourgeois, of the child, of the monk, or that of the soldier at war. The writers issued from Rousseauism could only conceive man as happy on an island. The localization of time resulting from the constancy of the conditions of a life submitted to the rhythm of the eternal return of the seasons as well as localization in space, tend to make the peasant live more in the duration of the species than in the time of the individual. From whence it comes that rural life remains the sanctuary of the immemorial and of tradition so long as the civilization of the cities does not intrude upon it to hasten its rhythm of time.   It is the theme of one of Charles Péguy's finest poems :

" He tenderly salutes the new time when he will be no longer.
When he will not be.
When his children will be.
The reign of his children.
He thinks with tenderness of that time which will no longer be his time.
But the time of his children.
The reign (of the time) of his children.
In that time when one shall say the Sevin and it will no longer mean him, but them.
Without more ado, without any explanation. " (1)

The darting of the gaze towards the horizon which, by projecting our imagination out of the space we have lived in produces in us the notion of futurity, evokes in modern man the melancholy sentiment of the shortness of life.   Therefore the sensation of space occasions in us a more acute consciousness of the flight of time.   The romantic landscape painters, and amongst them one must, of course, include the great romanticists of the xviith century such as Ruysdael, and in a certain measure Claude, have expressed this feeling of the flight of time by that *échappée* on to distant vistas which opens up in the background of their pictures.   One could say with Oswald Spengler that for them the third dimension blends with the fourth.   Most often this gap in the horizon allows us to assist at the great tragedy of the decline of light at the fall of day, — a poignant symbol of ephemeral life.   Introduced into Art by Giorgione, the moving consciousness of this drama will not cease to torment man until Chateaubriand.   It would seem as if Atala's " golden bar on the horizon " had become for us the symbol of our destiny.   But we have not yet reached the time when man lingers before the nostalgia of the sunset.   The Quattrocento artist who is not tormented by concern for the becoming, conceives space in a corporeal way : he delineates it and constructs it exactly like an architecture.   Yet by his perspectives he traces the beginning of the avenue that will eventually lead the modern painter out of near-by spaces, in which everything radiates with human presence, towards fatidical *lointains*.   Fra Angelico however expresses in a particularly frank manner his own conception of time which confounds itself with eternity.   He represents space like an hemisphere, sometimes like a complete circle, as in his *Coronations* of the Virgin.   The eye having travelled over the curve of space is brought back to its starting point in an endless gravitation, — the very image of the perfect movement which theologians ascribe to the contemplative soul...

The illusion of happiness is grasped by man in all that awakens in him the feeling of escaping from " the rustling loom of time " (2).   In the peasant's consciousness, the instinct of descent abolishes the anguish of the perishable.   It is in transcendency that the monk acquires the notion of eternity.   Lovers also, in the rapture which unites them, believe that they can elude destiny; perhaps because the generative act (which, whether it be deferred or not, remains the obscure goal of love) strikes a spark of eternity in their soul, as if the awakening of the species masked in their joined beings the consciousness of the ephemeral.   The contemplative act, which plunges each being into rapture with regard to the other, stops the single course of thought and fixes it in a gravitation which revolves around two foci, as in an ellipse.   An awkward curve, the utmost limit of human endeavour to attain harmony by earthly means alone, while the true symbol of divine love is the circumference.   All the yearning of the mystics tends to absorb one focus in the other and reduce the elliptical warping to circular perfection, in a flash of ecstasy, the soul being absorbed in God.   A bipolar figure, the ellipse is a symbol of tension; and tension is the law of all things created; it holds sway over the degradation of energy and over the celestial mechanics.   Is there a divine mechanics, regulated by the circular theme, in which all would be nothing but the emanation

---

(1) Charles Péguy : *Le Bûcheron.*
(1) *Faust*, by Goethe.

of a single focus of spiritual energy whose radiance would be similar to the propagation of waves spreading in concentric circles ? It would be the supreme state of the created, absorbed into the Increate, an absolute universe no longer ruled by the principle of the degradation of energy, the source of forces being none other than the Infinite itself. Is it towards this state of divine inertia that the agonizing " growth of entropy " is leading the world ?

*
* *

There once happened to be a monk endowed with genius who expressed in forms that sanctified hedonism of conventual life. A morning spent in leisurely meditation in the little cells of St. Mark enraptures the soul with the feeling of living outside of time. And indeed those frail figures are the very image of the bliss in which existed the angelic soul of a monk who, having realized the ideal of perfection in himself, having destroyed to their very roots all personal desire and will, felt liberated from the painful subjection of time.

The monasteries of the Middle-Ages are closely linked up with the general movement of civilization. They cooperated to it powerfully after having been its sole depositories. Above the immense crowd of monks who disappeared into conventual anonymity certain great adventurers of the spirit sprung up in the heart of the cloisters and launched out into the unknown of knowledge : St. Anselm, St. Thomas Aquinas, St. Francis of Assisi, Bacon... The golden age of claustral life was to end in the xvth century. Then the cloisters are merely associated with the life of the Church; they saw their emancipatory virtue disappear, but witnessed the continuation of the rôle of peaceful sanctuaries open to all refugees fleeing from the world and seeking happiness in renouncement. To-day they have become encysted in civilization like islets preserved from the general laws of evolution; they belong to another system of gravitation than that of the modern world. On entering a cloister the man of the world who is preoccupied by the problems of our epoch has rather the impression of accomplishing a wonderful journey into time. Even in the bosom of the Church itself monasteries tend to become isolated. Secular life is indifferent to them, when not actively hostile. Modern cloisters make one think of the neo-Gothic churches of Viollet-le-Duc.

The art of Fra Angelico represents in western civilization the last conjunction between the world and the cloister. Closely associated with the artistic evolution of his time, to such a degree even that it is quite impossible to form a just idea of painting during the Quattrocento if one does not ascribe to his the place that it deserves, the angelic friar has expressed in a synthesis of beauty a mystic tension capable of elevating the souls of his brethren, and a plastic ideal capable of filling with delectation the esthetic sense of a Medici. Many times in the history of forms, a religious ideal has found the means of expressing itself outside of classicism. Is it a mere chance that the Beau Dieu of Amiens seems, spanning the centuries, to belong to the same race as the Zeus by Phidias ? The serenity which the fixity of dogmas and precepts provides is a state of mind favourable to the elaboration of classical canons. Reciprocally, this form of art is the only one fit to translate the harmony of a religion which has reached the phase of maturity at the very moment it is still for man a means of defining himself and not a doctrine or an ethics which impose themselves to him as an intellectual and moral obligation. The classic cadence of Fra Angelico contains at the same time the glowing maturity of a religious civilization the decadence of which will soon be hastened by its historic destiny, and the radiant youth of a culture which enjoys the pure enthusiasm of a soaring. All this united in the soul of the frate by the seraphic candour of love which refuses to see any difference between beings and things, but rather discovers in each of them an aspect of that harmony which is eternal. Thus, by a signal grace, diverse currents converge in the soul of the blessed frate to make of his art a form of the cult paid to Beauty. In him rises joyfully a song of love uttered by the creature marvelling that its creator has made it so beautiful; the work of Fra Angelico is the last stanza of the long poem on the beauty of the world, — that image of divine splendour, — of which the zitherist of Assisi wrote the first strains. But the contemplation of his art elevates the spirit above the visible world to attain the vision of a more abstract beauty. The soul, feeling itself an instant liberated from carnal chains, and freed from the laws of destiny, feels itself transported far beyond the perishable into a better world where the sad old man armed with a scythe reigns no longer. It deludes itself with the " intemporal " dream indulged in by

Plato : " Think what happiness would be man's if he could see the beautiful itself unalloyed and in lieu of a beauty burdened with flesh, with colours and a hundred other perishable superfluities, contemplate divine beauty itself in its unique form. "

Limpid reflection of beauty in the mirror of a soul which has transported into its vision of the temporal world the serenity of that which lives outside of time, — such a harmony could indeed only be born in a cloister ! The cloister is as much as the cathedral one of those essential creations by which the spirit of the West has revealed itself. The one completes the other. The cathedral is altitude, whereas the cloister is gravitation. There is some truth in Viollet-le-Duc's theory concerning the lay character of cathedrals. Those prodigious structures born of a lyrical *élan* were not made for monks; archeologists bring us the proof of this by telling us that the Gothic cathedral has its origin in that type of Romanesque church called " pilgrimage ". It is the impulse of the people which enlarged the church rendering it superhuman, huge, infinite. The symphony of the cathedral which is a limitless exhaustion of space in the vibration of light, is romantic and Wagnerian in essence. The harmony of the cloisters in its principle is similar to that of classical music founded on the feeling of plenitude caused in the soul by the " eternal return " of a melody, the harmonious outline of which has aroused in the soul the nostalgia of happiness. Thanks to this cyclical rhythm, the composer neutralizes the poignant effect of the music to which our soul is so sensitive, because alone, of all the arts, its domain is time and not space.

Side by side with the huge cathedral, — that projection into space of a soul tormented by its yearning for the divine, the cloister is the image of that serenity conquered through faith. Western architecture has often associated these two elements : the cloister rests in the shade of the cathedral; in a single monument are united the most typical expression of the becoming to the most poetic image of eternity ! Shut off from space and the world by the screen of its seclusion, the true aspect of the cloister, like all that the Middle-Ages have created, like their stained glass windows and their illuminations, is from within. It opens wide its arcades on to a few square feet of an area where a garden, disposed around a well-kerb, assembles all that since the origins of christianity resumes for man the image of paradise : seclusion, verdure, light, freshness of flowing water and of shade. *Hortus conclusus.* A garden shut off from space as from time, whose quadrature begets the circle without either beginning or ending, marvelous image of the infinite circumscribed within the limit; of the universal in one.

MICHELOZZO. Cloister of St. Antoninus.
Convent of San Marco, Florence.

Unfailing beauty of western cloisters ! Perfect definition of Romanesque cloisters in which the circular theme is enriched by the semi-circle ! Prodigality of the Clunisians who offer a universe of forms to the imagination retrenched from the world. Sublime abstraction of the Cistercians who, disdaining circumlocutions, place the soul directly in front of the terrible exaction that it should be itself in integral nakedness. Palestrinian lyricism of the Gothic cloister; the fugal style of the small arcades of the cloister of Mont Saint-Michel, suspended like an aerie above the infinite ! The sweet scent of southern cloisters where one breathes the fragrance of *garrigues* burnt by the sun; the watery smell of cloisters of the North, situated in the hollow of sylvan valleys; the classical cadence of the cloisters of Saint-Maur, whose exact Doric columns invite one to study and to a logical course of thought; the desperate lyricism of the Franciscan cloisters : is not the *Sacro Convento* of Assisi a veritable symphony of cloisters ? There one finds the cloister which reconquered by the world has become a square, a parvis, rather than a cloister, and which, like the atrium of primitive basilicas, offers itself like a promise and invites one to purification; then comes the great cloister opening on to an enclosure paved with sun and shadow; its superposed galleries evoke an amphi-theatre built to allow one to contemplate the play of light on the diamond of the chevet of the basilica : on the flank of the *convento* clings a two storied belvedere like an imperfect cloister suspended over the valley : it is here that the monks conduct their guests at the decline of daylight in order that they may enjoy that softness which Umbrian evenings shed upon humans affected by the burning day ! And lastly there is the mystery of the cloisters of the dead overrun by a wild vegetation which hides within its sacred soil not mortals but elect, out of each of whom a cypress has grown...

More simple, more secret perhaps is in Florence that luminous aerie whose center was cooled by the shade of a cypress, and girdled by a simple ring of arcades, the joyous rhythm of which unrolls like the round of angels and elect which unfolds on a small panel in the neigh-bouring penumbra of the *ospizio* :

Una ruota se fa in cielo
Dalli Santi in quel giardino...

San Marco, divine cloister where a brother lived the promise of bliss contained in the VIth Beatitude :

Blessed are the pure in heart for they shall see God.

THE ARTIST

No school of art has been as much as the Italian school sheltered from the effects of the influences and vicissitudes of history. It is wonderful to see how, once its starting capital was constituted at the end of the xiiith century, it follows a process of unfailing internal development which leads to Giotto and to Tintoretto. Jacob Burckhardt has rather strained the sense of this movement by transferring to its origin the modern notion of " revolution " which has quickened the course of civilization since the Reformation and which, in the xixth century, became the principle of all creation.

During all the Western period which extends from the origins to the xvith century, in spite of the endemic violence which reigned in events, the general evolution of civilization took place like an organic development according to a vital process. The ferment of novation brought by St. Francis of Assisi, — a new Christ, — is at least as important in its multiple consequences as that which Luther will reveal to the world. Yet the latter is a revolutionary, the former not. The essential reform which the *poverello* imposed upon human sensibility was accomplished without a shock. The principle of individualism he brought to the world penetrated harmoniously into the frame of mediaeval collectivism which its development was to shiver one day. Likewise in the xiith century, the rise of the commons which, however, manifested itself under a " revolutionary " aspect, was canalized and integrated by the Capetian monarchy into the social and political order.

Italian art reveals its rhythm only when one envisages it as a unity extending from the xiith to the xvith century. The revolutionary aspect which may strike one at the beginning of the xvth century, when one compares the productions of that period with its immediate antecedents, fades away if one links up the great creators of the Quattrocento directly with those of the Trecento. There is not, properly speaking, a revolution but a resumption of the original creative activity, after one of those moments of decadence or of depression which are always the consequence of a great creative period, and which, in art, breeds academism. Thus Masaccio naturally " continues " Giotto, whilst as Mr. Emilio Cecchi has remarked very justly, an artist like Andrea del Castagno draws his profound ascendancy from a certain Tuscan tradition of which Pietro Lorenzetti was, in the Middle-Ages, the most remarkable instance. The sad decadence of which Tuscany gave the example at the end of the xivth century at a time when Northern Italy was in full activity, masked that harmonious continuity and authorised historians to speak of Renaissance and of Revolution.

The old centenarian gothico-giottesque tree had survived until the beginning of the xvth century; there are few spectacles as tiring in the history of art than all those works by Spinello Aretino, Giovanni del Biondo, Mariotto di Nardo, Pari Spinelli, Agnolo Gaddi, Niccolo di Pietro, Gerini, whose panels clutter up the museums, and whose frescoes decorate the Churches of Tuscany. After the " genesis " which had ended in the creation of Italian painting, Italy catching up with the general evolution of European art which she was a century behind, had entered into academism. Giotto Duccio and Simone had supplied all the xivth century; these sources were sufficiently abundant to allow the Florentine and Sienese schools, by placing their heritage in common, to preserve a vital tonus sufficient to produce painters of real merit, especially at Siena. At the beginning of the xvth century, these same sources were drained. Siena counts hardly any painters; Florence still possesses a prosperous school at least as far as the number of artists, the abundance of production, and the fixity of its dogmas, are concerned : but its painters follow merely the manual and mental automatisms of a sterile scholasticism. An immense ennui seems to weigh upon this senile art as one can see from the tired attitudes, the dull eyes, the sullen faces, the flagging and empty forms, the vacillating compositions, the grimacing draperies devoid of all style, true caricatures of that art of the drapery which Giotto and Simone had carried to so great a power of expression. If one compares these works with those of Giotto's direct disciples such as Bernardo Daddi, Taddeo Gaddi, and the Lorenzetti, one notices that this regression in the art of painting is marked by a progression of linearism at the expense of the modelling. French miniature at the epoch of Charles V underwent a similar crises of caricatural graphism before being regenerated by Lombard influence and by Flemish contributions. Because they no longer feel the life of the form in space, Giotto's followers, at the beginning of the xvth century, replace a " transition " by a linear demarcation but this line does not possess the plastic intensity of a Japanese arabesque, or of nervous contour by Jean Pucelle or Pisanello who, in their " limit " express the truth of a body; it is merely a soft undulation or a sharp zigzag such as children trace; it only recovers sometimes a little tone when the hand that is guiding it has a senile contraction, chafing at its powerlessness.

According to whether they proceed from a renewal of vigour in a felled trunk, or that, being entirely new creations, they spring directly from a seed, the language of foresters separates young trees into stock-shoots or seed lips. These two expressions might well define the respective positions od Don Lorenzo Monaco and of Fra Angelico, with regard to the gothico-giottesque stock. To the continual repetition of the old vocabulary the camaldolite monk brings a naiveté of heart and a freshness of soul which restores a moment of life to that dead art. Perhaps he discovered this Fountain of Youth in miniature, an art of which the limited perspective, the patient execution, and the confidential character are well suited to the peace of the cloisters. Under Don Lorenzo Monaco's impulsion a center of miniaturists was developed at the Convent of St. Mary of the Angels; from this center came the best illuminated books of a school which was not conspicuous in this art. Don Lorenzo Monaco tried around about 1400, to reform the school on lines which had been realized towards 1350 by the Di Cione brothers Jacopo and Andréa Orcagna; he restored tension to the relaxed line, style to the draperies, intensity to the colour. Between the two traditions, — that of Giotto and the Sienese, which had been supplying the pictural needs of Florence for the last fifty yeurs, he inclines resolutely towards the second. Did he not rediscover in his best works such as the *Annunciation*, of the Academy of Florence, the graceful flexibility of Simone's line ? Doubtless it was he who drewthe attention of young Guido di Pietro to Sienese mysticism ?

The articulation of the link which Don Lorenzo Monaco forms between the painting of the xivth century and Fra Angelico, is a proof of the logical continuation of the evolution of Italian painting. Don Lorenzo came just in time to restore a little vigour to tradition, so as to allow the art of Guido di Pietro to feed upon a living humus and not upon an exhausted soil. The statement according to which our painter would have been formed at the school of the problematic Starnina is rejected by all. Although we possess no precisions in this respect, no historian doubts today but that the dominican monk received lessons from the camaldolite. It is more than likely that this happened when the Dominicans of Fiesole returned from their exile at Cortona i.e. in 1418. The recent historians of Fra Angelico are indeed almost agreed to admit that his career is a tardy vocation dating only from about 1420-1425. The following remark may confirm this hypothesis. The Reliquary of the Museum of St. Mark in Florence showing the *Annunciation* and the *Adoration of the Magii* (see plate 53), must be posterior to 1423, date of the *Adoration of the Magii*, painted by Gentile di Fabiano for Santa Trinita, which picture was to become immediately one of the most popular of the time. The group of Joseph and Mary and that of the Wise Men in Adoration are very alike in both works. The Magian who is prostrate, one hand resting upon the ground whilst his back is almost horizontal, seems indeed to have been borrowed by Fra Angelico from Gentile's picture (1).

The reliquary of Santa Maria Novella with its gold background decorated with guilloches, with the unreal aspect of its tapering forms derived from the Gothic, reveals the formation of the miniaturist. By its preciosity this work makes one think more of a Persian miniature than of a Gothic illumination. This is also the case of the *Madonna* of the Vatican Museum (Plates 57 and 60). The Virgins of the Museum of St. Mark (Pl. 58 and 62), of the Rijksmuseum (Pl. 59 and 63), and of San Domenico of Cortona (Pl. 67 and 68), which appear to be posterior still belong to the Gothic-Giotto lineage. They possess that robust pyramidal balance of which Bernardo Daddi had laid the foundations of the tradition in the school; the bust of the Virgin is placed, as on a socle, on the legs which are wrapped in the draperies of Gothic folds. The Madonna of St. Mark reproduces almost feature for feature a Virgin by Don Lorenzo Monaco. She might be a little posterior to the one of Cortona, for she attests a progress in the expression of volume and emancipation from miniature, as is shown in particular by the very exact drawing of the hands. As for the Madonna of the Rijksmuseum, she must belong to the period of maturity. All these different Virgins stand out against backgrounds of flowered draperies " guilloched " with gold, which confer them that aspect of painted gems of the reliquary of Santa Maria Novella.

The Coronation of the Virgin of the Museum of St. Mark, is Fra Angelico's first attempt to solve the problem of space (Pl. 61, 64, 65 and 66). This work is turned resolutely towards the future. Instead of disposing the personages of a scene upwards on a scaffolding, as the painters of the xivth century had done, Fra Angelico situates them in depth. One need only compare this picture to that on the same subject painted by Don Lorenzo Monaco which is in the Uffizi Gallery, to realize the enormous progress which had been accomplished in a few years. In spite of their crescent-shaped disposition, the Camaldolite's personages remain inert on a single plane. Fra Angelico's composition, on the other hand, describes a great harmonious orb in space; a few angels move with ease in the depth of the picture and by the suppleness and mobility of their draperies, they recall certain of Ghiberti's personages; the gradual diminution of the figures according to the distance, is well observed; nevertheless they preserve the elongated proportions and the conventional folds of Gothic tradition; a few awkward touches are also noticeable, and no doubt one should already discern the hand of an aid in this exquisite work.

This picture also attracts us by the fresh and dainty éclat of its colours which stand out against a golden background. All his life Fra Angelico will employ with love an harmony of tender colours made up of lilac, mauve, pink, water-green, bright yellow, light azure, orange and delicate lacquers. This tradition of the harmony of half-tones goes back to antiquity itself. It seems to have been conceived by Hellenic Painting; it was, in any case, used in the most ancient Alexandrian illuminations which have come down to us, — such as the *Genesis* of Vienna, of the vth century. This joyous chromatism sings in the oldest Byzantine mosaics, those of the vth century at Santa Maria Maggiore, at the Orthodoxes, and at the Mausoleum of Galla Placidia at Ravenna, — whilst the mosaics of the vith century, such as those of Saint Apollinarius, are already touched by that darkening of colour particular to the East. This Hellenistic tradition of colour will be faithfully preserved by Byzantine miniature; it shines in all its brillance in the Paris *Psalter* of the xth century, a late masterpiece of Alexandrian art. In the West, the same current feeds certain schools of Carolingian miniature, and also of Ottonian miniature which later proceeds from it. However the painting of Romanesque France is divided between the use of light colour of Hellenic origin, and the Eastern style of dull tones which makes a great use of dark reds, grenats, browns, hard blues, and ochreous or earthy tones. The illumination which flourished in France in the xiiith century tends more towards Eastern colouring, being founded on an harmony of dark blue and brownish red which will even be transposed to stained-glass windows. This is equally true of the Italian painting of the " Dugento " which seems to imitate Cappadocian paintings. Yet half-tone chromatism flourished again in Duccio, who feeds on Byzantine substance and is, from many points

---

(1) The aged Magian kissing the foot of the Child who blesses him appeared for the first time in Italian art at the beginning of the xivth century, under the influence of the meditations of the pseudo Bonaventurae. But he is always simply kneeling. In *Les Très Riches Heures* of the Duc de Berry (between 1411 and 1416) he is already represented with one hand placed on the ground. Gentile pictures him prostrate, attitude which the enigmatical author of the *Adoration of the Magii* of the Berlin Museum also repeats. This work is perhaps due to a Florentine imitating Pisanello round about 1450.

of view, the last of the Alexandrians. Thanks to Duccio's impulsion, this tradition will become very firmly established in Sienese painting. Simone di Martino, Pietro Lorenzetti, do not deviate from it. But at the end of the xivth century, the abstract colouring of Giotto's followers reigns in Siena and in Florence, whilst Lombardesque miniature diffused throughout the whole of Europe under the name of " work of Lombardy " the light tones of the Alexandrian scale of colours. At the beginning of the xvth century, Don Lorenzo Monaco restored this tradition in Florence, and the dark modelling of his flesh tints which he has retained from Giotto, contrast strangely with the glad freshness of his colours. It is to the Camaldolite monk that Fra Angelico owes this coloured harmony which he will use all his life, even in the most monumental compositions, such as those of the studio at the Vatican to which those light and lovely tints are hardly suited. He will also be the last to employ them. Thus a tradition several centuries old will die with him.

By the way it is conceived, not in the plan but in space, the *Coronation of the Virgin* of the Museum of St. Mark, really belongs to the Renaissance; it is surprizing that certain historians have not grasped its innovating element. The works now presented to us and which form a coherent group, show us Fra Angelico voluntarily devoted to the spirit which is that of a painter of the Quattrocento. These works are the *Annunciation* of Cortona (Pl. 69 to 71), — the *Coronation of the Virgin* of the Louvre (Pl. 72 to 77), — the *Madonna of the Linaiuoli* (Pl. 78 to 81), — the *Polyptych* of Perugia (Pl. 84, 86, 87). The *Madonna of the Linaiuoli* gives us a date : 1433. The Madonna of Perugia was painted in 1437. The Annunciation and the Coronation must have been painted between these two dates; I would even willingly believe that these two pictures are contemporary. All the paintings we have just mentioned are the work of an artist who has reached maturity. However there still subsists in the *Madonna of the Linaiuoli* a certain awkwardness which results perhaps from the unusual dimensions of the panel. As for the Annunciation of Cortona it is no doubt the most perfect of all Fra Angelico's works.

In all these pictures the artist seems touched by the prestige which, immediately after their execution in 1427, the frescoes of the Brancacci Chapel of the Carmine of Florence exerted upon the painters of the Quattrocento. Masaccio was the true emancipator of Fra Angelico who was still hesitating between Giotto and Gothicism. Like the master of the Brancacci Chapel, the painter of the *Coronation of the Virgin* seemed uniquely preoccupied by the manner of expressing volumes in space. Reduced to their essential modelling, the bodies he paints " turn ". Compared to the Angel of the reliquary of Santa Maria Novella that of Cortona shows us the transition between the Middle-Ages and the Renaissance. His is a regularly constituted body and no longer a mere form tapering like a spindle. The folds of the draperies fall in flutings and abandon the curvilineal flourishes of Gothic calligraphy. The *Coronation of the Virgin* of the Louvre continues this sculptural progression to the point of bringing the artist to retract the purely spatial version of that of St. Mark. The picture presents some resemblance to a bas-relief and all the personages are conceived in a statuary spirit : the Virgin alone preserves the tapering canon symbol of the effusion of the soul which is that of the statues of the Royal Portal of Chartres. Nevertheless of the two sensations which express the idea of body, — that of volume and that of weight, — Fra Angelico retains only the first. He preserves something of Gothic unreality and by a curious antinomy constructs bodies having a well delimited volume in space which, however, seem transparent; the volume is reduced to a corporeal envelope without density. One is hardly surprised to see his personages rise up into the air; they do not appear to obey the laws of gravitation but rather those of an attraction of the light which transcends them. At the same time as he acquires this new sentiment of volume, Fra Angelico investigates more deeply his experience in space. Like the other painters of his generation, he considers it as a body, that is to say as a closed and strictly delimitated universe. However, rather than escape into perspective, he prefers the limitation of space pursuant to the curve of a half-circle thus solving the problem of depth while preserving a perfect rhythmical unity to the picture. The *Coronation* of the Louvre, like that of the museum of St. Mark, goes so far as to suggest the idea of the complete circle surrounding the central group in a ring placed in perspective. This mode of composition, founded on the impression of harmony which the image of the circle procures to the eye, will become almost systematic with Fra Angelico until the epoch of his Vatican work. This plastic design led him at least as much as the mystical idea, to conceive the composition of the *Sacra Conversazione* which will have so great a success in the Italian School which came after him.

The works of this period reveal a painter who has escaped from the arbitrary of tradition and who discovers the reality of the exterior world. They manifest certain traits of sensibility one would find in no contemporary, such as the delicate tracery of blue veins visible on the hands of the Saints of the retable of Perugia (Pl. 87) or of certain personages of the *Descent from the Cross* of the Museum of St. Mark (Pl. 89-93).

This last picture seems to be slightly posterior. It reveals the collaboration of the fresco painters of the Convent of St. Mark, and is the work of an artist completely liberated from school conventions who recreates an original plastic world from elements entirely borrowed from the real. This painting, the expression of which is perhaps not particularly prepossessing, is probably the master's finest, best balanced composition, as well as the largest, thanks to the vast landscape which blends synthetically two types of Italian nature : the *contado*, and the *municipe*.

Studio of Fra Angelico. THE ARREST OF CHRIST.
Convent of San Marco, Florence. Cell 33.

In vain would one seek in the Italian painting of the Quattrocento for an artist having so direct a sentiment of Nature as Fra Angelico. The Florentine painters of that century discarded the old landscape conventions on which the school had been living for more than a hundred years, but they substituted to them others which although deduced from the study of nature, are none the less arbitrary. Alone amongst them the blessed friar casts upon nature a candid and moved gaze. His small landscapes are full of elements which have been observed by an eye more sensitive than curious. Behind the *Visitation* in the predella of the *Annunciation* of Cortona opens a horizon a few centimeters large (Pl. 85), in which one glimpses in the distance the shining light of Lake Trasimena, is in the history of painting, one of the first landscapes in which the subject is identifiable. We shall have to wait four centuries before finding again in the person of Corot as sensitive an observer of the Tuscan and Umbrian countryside.

Fra Angelico shares with Corot a same ingenuousness of the eye and a very delicate sentiment of the values of atmosphere absolutely unknown to his contemporaries whose geometrical, statufied, and stuffy landscapes seem to belong to some other planet rather than to our own. This subtle sense of atmosphere and of depth which is not represented by perspective but by values, does not abandon Fra Giovanni when he paints an indoor space; he has known how to render as no other artist of his time the soft light, the passages by degrees and halftones from light to shadow, which are peculiar to indoor lighting; one can safely say that in all circumstances, whether it be in outdoor scenes or in scenes of intimacy, he has revealed himself as delicate a luminist as a Dutch painter. He has indeed inherited from the Middle-Ages that aesthetics which confounded beauty and light; such pictures as the *Annunciation* of Cortona, or the *Coronation of the Virgin* of the Louvre irradiate light.

Fra Angelico's qualities as a landscape painter were those which his pupils were best able to assimilate. How many times in works which bear no trace of his hand do we discover those vistas in which one suddenly has the impression of recognizing the precious rareness of his personal art ? (Pl. 166 and 173).

These characteristics of sensitive observation are especially noticeable in the predellas of the great altar-pieces. Two predellas which he himself executed after 1430 have been preserved for us : that of the *Annunciation* of Cortona (Pl. 85, 94 and 95), and that of the *Coronation of the Virgin* at the Louvre (Pl. 96 to 103). It can be said that this artist's genius changes of aspect according as he works on the space of a picture or on that of a predella. There are there two different scales to which the painter adapts himself with a remarkable facility. In the great altar tables, largely composed, he satisfies the plastic and monumental instincts of a Quattrocentist haunted by the idea of volume; and the art of the sculptor is an example for him. In the predellas, on the contrary, he adopts a narrative style better suited to the hagiographic legends he narrates. There he gives free rein to his effusions. One could almost in a way say that he is Florentine in the retables and Sienese in the predellas. And yet these small figures which seem conceived on the scale of miniatures, possess in themselves a monumentality which is revealed by enlargement as I have been able to ascertain by having macrophotographs of the predella of the *Coronation of the Virgin* and of the *Martyrdom of St. Cosmas and St. Damian* (Pl. 133 to 150), made in the Laboratory of the Louvre. Under the magnifying lens such a face which, to normal vision, appears treated with the minutia of a miniaturist's brush, suddenly assumes the majesty of one of Masaccio's figures.

When after having studied all these harmonious and joyful works, one passes to the frescoes of the Convent of St. Mark which follow them (Pl. 104 to 131), one is struck by the accent of austerity of the latter. It almost seems as if the artist had submitted his painting to a claustral retreat. He rediscovers Giotto's renouncement and severity. In the history of Italian painting Giotto appears to us less as an individual than as a principle. I do not know if any other artist has ever expressed as strongly as he has the genius of a people; — Phidias perhaps. The return to Giotto's spirit whether it be conscious or not signifies for Italian painting the return to its source. One discovers traces of Giotto even in Caravaggio, and at the end of the evolution, even in Piazetta.

Beyond Giotto the style of the frescoes of St. Mark make one think of the great monumental parts of French sculpture of the xiiith century. These figures reduced to a few unities are disposed against a neutral background as against that of a bas-relief. The fall of the drapery is nearer to Gothic cadence than to that of Giotto. The serenity and impersonality of the faces recall also the Saints of French Cathedrals. A figure like that of *Christ Mocked* (Pl. 117) really finds its companion only in the French art of the xiiith century; it evokes the Christs of certain Last Judgments, whilst that of the *Transfiguration* (Pl. 118) is an anticipation of Raphael. Before the *Coronation of the Virgin* (Pl. 124) memory reverts to the same subject treated in the Portal of the Virgin at Notre-Dame, in Paris. As for the *Madonna* in the corridor (Pl. 109), it is connected with a still far more distant past as we shall see in the following chapter. The frescoes, — by far the most numerous, — which have been executed by pupils less freed from tradition than their master, possess a more Giotto-like character (Pl. 169 to 176). In St. Mark this renascent Gothic classicism is the sign of Fra Angelico's personal style. It seems rather deliberate, for other works painted on panels at the same period, such as the *Descent from the Cross* (Pl. 89 to 93), have much more in common with the spirit of the time. This last picture does not recall French sculpture but rather the Florentine sculpture of the epoch, of which it imitates the rhythms and modelling.

From the frescoes of Orvieto (Pl. 142 and 143), executed in 1447, Fra Angelico's art appears to undergo a very decided change of direction. His style becomes more ample but also looser, a non equivocal sign of the influence of the Eternal City which few artists who have sojourned there have ever escaped. At this contact the painter from Fiesole will lose some of his native qualities. He is attracted by the sense of grandeur, but he also abandons that compact, precise, flawless style, that " *ostinato rigore* ", which is the *grâce d'état* of

Studio of Fra Angelico. THE BEARING OF THE CROSS, Fresco.
Convent of San Marco, Florence. Cell 28.

Tuscan painters. He is touched by that banality of form which all Roman painters will know. The research for more majestuous volumes *à la romaine*, leads him to abdicate that delicacy of line, that concision of modelling, which conferred so high a plastic and spiritual distinction to the first part of his work. Fra Angelico is no longer related to Giotto but to Cavallini, the founder of the tradition of Roman painting. The figures of St. Bonaventura (Pl. 154) and of the Pontiff (Pl. 155) evoke the frescoes of St. Cecilia at the Transtevere; unfortunately, if they possess the amplitude of the latter, they lack their power.

The admirable synchronism between plastic expression and the religious subject which formed the elevation of this art, also disappears towards this epoch. Fra Angelico appears uniquely preoccupied by plastic problems. As he grows older has the monk sacrificed without realizing it to the Pagan gods of the Renaissance ? The frescoes of the " studio " of Nicholas V at the Vatican (Pl. 144 to 156), which must have been executed during Fra Angelico's second stay in Rome, after 1452, strike us by the importance of their architectures; the personages seem to be there merely to fill in the fabrics. On arriving in Rome the artist was enthralled by the grandeur of the antique and Christian monuments. The architectural style of his Roman works deviates from the fine style of Michelozzo whose cristalline rhythms the *frate* formerly took pleasure in reproducing; it already announces that, of a very vigorous rhythm more directly inspired from antiquity, of the eldest of the San Gallo, — Giuliano. The oldest works of this Florentine architect who elaborated some of the values from which Bramante and the architecture of the XVIth century were to emerge, are twenty years posterior. Thus Fra Angelico cuts in a sense the figure of a precursor. At this period architecture appears to be his chief preoccupation. He even sacrifices to it space so dear to Florentines. It is indeed remarkable that in these Vatican scenes the artist completely abandons amphitheatrical compositions for which he had shown such an exclusive predilection during the first part of his career. His personages are now disposed against backgrounds of architecture like actors on the restricted space of a stage. There is no longer, properly speaking, any depth, but an architectural surface of a rich decorative effect, which clothes gorgeously the wall rather than it animates it by a stage setting *plaqué à la romaine*. Instead of being apportioned according to those harmonious proportions of which the Master of the Convent of St. Mark had the secret, the space is filled up rather clumsily and without rhythm (see Plate 153). Certain forms attain that expression of Roman majesty which the artist was seeking, but it is at the expense of balance and cadence. One need only compare a figure like that of the High Priest in the *Judgment of St. Stephen* (Pl. 152); with the *Christ Mocked* of St. Mark's (Pl. 117), to realize the declines which appears in the painter's style of that epoch.

The comparison of the two great *Holy Conversations* which are to be found in the Museum of St. Mark, throws light upon the transformation which then takes place in the art of Fra Angelico. The now very deteriorated work which used formerly to decorate the high altar of the convent church (Pl. 138), is one of the artist's masterpieces. Conceived no doubt shortly before his departure for Rome, it marks the culminating point of the Florentine period. Once again the artist draws an admirable concertant harmony from the theme of circular composition. Grouped around the Virgin, the Saints and angels form a choir from which a song of joy rises in unison; the composition possesses the perfection and gives the impression of beatitude of a cantata by Palestrina; the festoons, the curtains and the reveals by means of which the artist rounds off the straight lines and the angles, accompany the circular theme which is the subject of the picture. In the background a marvelous garden closes the open space with a live hedge through which one catches a glimpse of the horizon. The picture of the Franciscan convent called " *Bosco di Frati* " (Pl. 139) which was painted during the roman period, is constructed according to radically different rules which announce the Cinquecento. As in the *Holy Conversations* of Fra Bartolommeo, of Bellini and Raphael, the Saints and angels tend to distribute themselves into two compact groups on each side of the Virgin. They are indeed obliged to do this on account of the restricted space allotted to them in front of the great monumental wall which closes brutally the picture. The task of expressing what remains of the circular theme is entrusted to the architecture. The niche which shelters the Virgin in the Dominicans' picture is still a cathedral niche designed according to human proportions, a tabernacle, a theme, a familiar object. In the Franciscans' picture, it forms part and parcel of the wall and widens into an hemicycle which announces the grandiose conception of Bramante at the Belvedere. Did Fra Angelico dream before Bramante in front of the great exedra of the Flavians on the Palatine? The personages of the last named picture are no more than figurantes; in the altar of St. Mark they are the composition itself, whereas here they merely enrich it. The Florentine picture conceived in spatial depth, and the beauty of which resides in the full use of the aesthetic, hedonistic, and beatific resources of the circular theme, is succeeded by the Roman picture conceived like an architecture which will triumph with the classicists of the XVIth century. Like in the case of the *School of Athens*, one imagines that the work could be sufficient in itself without the personages. The starting point of this transformation dates from 1450. In the first phase of Florentine painting of the Quattrocento, architecture merely lent the artist the perspective of its colonnades, contributing thus to the deepening of the effect to space. A little later it will present itself in width in the composition and close the picture with the density of a wall, like a bas-relief. Indeed Fra Angelico had been preceded in this conception by Fra Filippo Lippi. The Madonna which is to-day in the Uffizi Gallery, and which the latter artist painted in 1437 for Santa Croce, shows this wall as occupying the whole space of the picture, hollowed out with niches and scanned by columns in front of which the personages seem posed like so many statues.

Certain historians tend to attribute Fra Angelico's Roman decadence to the extensive collaboration of younger artists who reacted upon their old master, such as in particular, Benozzo Gozzoli. We will see later what one should think of this hypothesis. We have just spoken of the Madonna of the *Bosco di Frati*. Benozzo's collaboration may be envisaged in this picture but the want of firmness noticeable in this work is no doubt due to the exhaustion of the painting. Yet the panels which retrace the history of St. Cosmas and St. Damian, and of which one is not sure whether they formed or not part of the predella of the great Madonna of St. Mark's, seem to attest that Fra Angelico's art had not fallen into complete decadence during the roman period. They certainly belong to the latter as the architectures prove (Pl. 136). But being partially ruined these works have often been ill appreciated. Indeed the *Judgment* (Pl. 136) admits of certain weaknesses of execution, but the *Burial* (Pl. 137) is certainly one of the frate's finest works in spite of the clumsy retouches which mar it. One notices in it, as in the *Martyrdom* of the Louvre (Pl. 133), that rhythmical quality of well-distributed space, that sense of depth and of aerial surroundings, which are particular to Fra Giovanni's best works. In the *Martyrdom* which has come down to us almost intact, the figures possess the beauty and nobility of style of the artist's first period, as can be seen in the enlargement I have had made of one of them (Pl. 134).

It is certain that at that period the Master, who was no doubt weary, no longer worked much himself, as is proven by the execution of the *sportelli* of the *Annunziata*, which he entirely entrusted to his pupils.

Formed towards 1420, Fra Angelico found himself placed in a particularly favourable position to receive simultaneously the teachings and traditions which flowed towards him from Siena and Florence, and from the results of the first experiences realized by the Florentine sculptors. Starting from illumination and encouraged by Masaccio, he soon rejoined his contemporaries in that research of spatial values which was the great goal of that generation of painter-sculptors to which he belonged. However the passion of learning does not give his art that tension which contracts that of an Ucello or of a Castagno. In him traditions and novelties blend harmoniously together. He is the Tuscan artist *par excellence ;* no art in the Florence of the Quattrocento is more high spirited than his. His quarters of nobility are Cimabue, Giotto, Simone, and Andrea Pisano. Steeped in tradition he reaches immediately without fumbling the perfection of his art. A work like the *Annunciation* of Cortona is perhaps the summit of Tuscan painting. In the humble church of the Gesù, which opens on to a square full of light suspended above the sublime Val di Chiana, this picture shines with a rare éclat. To the visitor obsessed by this perfection, it would almost seem as if the whole of Cortona had, since the Etruscans, been conceived and had evolved merely in order that it might one day become the casket of this gem which occupies in Italian painting the radiant place filled in French painting by the *Madonna* of Antwerp, by Jean Fouquet. Like the latter work, it surpasses the simple definition of painting : it partakes of the nature of illumination of enamel, jewellery, architecture and sculpture. The elegant sureness of the arabesques, the masterly incisiveness of the line which only belongs to Tuscan art, the exact concision of volumes, the luminous intensity of colour, the rhythm of the architecture, the harmonious distribution of space, all make of it one of those flawless works which one cannot behold without emotion, for this perfection is the result of a long succession of centuries. It would seem as if generations and generations of artists had laboured throughout the ages to end in this supreme expression of a style. Giotto, and Simone, are present herein, and also a Gothic classicism, whilst spanning the centuries, that colouring, with its soft and saturated hues, seems to proceed directly from Alexandria. In that veritable Hellas which Tuscany was during the Quattrocento, Fra Angelico is Attic, whereas Masaccio is Spartan. Brother Angelico was so well identified with his native Tuscany that on leaving it he ceased to be himself. Rome proved fatal for him : it was there he lost the state of grace.

THE ARREST OF CHRIST. VIth century mosaic.
St. Apollinarius, Ravenna.

THE IMAGE MAKER

FOR Fra Angelico art does not carry its end in itself. It is at the service of the Idea which it translates by means of signs that render the mysteries of the Christian dogma perceptible to the senses. Isolated in the midst of the Renaissance, Fra Angelico remains an " image maker " for whom art is only a manifestation in the temporal world of transcendental values, a means of interpreting the invisible by the visible, the ineffable by what Dante termed the " *parlar visibile* ". It is therefore necessary if one wishes to obtain a just idea of the art of the Dominican monk, not to study his work from an exclusively plastic point of view, but to seek what may be its spiritual signification in the development of Christian thought.

That aspect of Fra Angelico's art has more than once tempted religious writers. The most remarkable of those studies are also the most ancient, those of the Dominicans, — of Father Marchese, and especially Father Boissel who have shown the relations of Fra Angelico's works with certain literary sources, both religious and profane, and with monastic customs. Well-informed as they may be, the interesting speculations of Canon Broussolle belong more to pious literature than to objective study. They are therefore not much help to the historian. In a general way, the defect of authors preoccupied by this question is to have deduced a personal interpretation from the paintings of Fra Angelico without taking into account the iconographic mediaeval traditions from which they spring. Yet it is if one studies it in function of these traditions that the *frate's* work assumes from a religious point of view a peculiar relief and reveals a profound originality. Such a study shows that he was indisputably the last representative of the sacred art of the Middle-Ages.

During the Middle-Ages, all Christian iconography oscillated between two tendencies, contained in principle in the very origins of Byzantine art : the pathetic expression and the theological signification. In his famous " *Recherches sur l'Iconographie de l'Evangile* " Gabriel Millet has analysed with many details the thousand fluctuations and the multiple interferences of the original iconographic themes. With that genius for synthesis which characterizes his talent as historian, Emile Magne has strongly opposed the theological so-called hellenistic tradition to the pathetic tradition considered as having originated in Syria. For each Gospel scene he has reduced the prototypes to two opposed versions, which he considers as being the source of all the western interpretations. In a general way, and by taking a very simplified view of things, one can say that the Church of the East gave preponderance to the theological version, whilst that of the West inclined more willingly towards the pathetic.

The theological interpretation triumphs however in the Occident with the French religious art of the xiiith century which transposes into the world of forms the symbolic and ordered universe conceived by scholastic thinkers. But under the influence of Franciscan spirituality, Italy was soon to substitute to that intellectual iconography a wholly sensible interpretation of Gospel scenes which would transpose into religious art the passions of the human heart : suffering, tenderness, and love. A book like *Meditations on the Life of Christ*, written in the xiiith century by an unknown franciscan and which was then thought to be by St. Bonaventura, touches the Christian's heart by descriptions which appeal to sentiments he has experienced; it testifies to the progress of anthropomorphism over theocentrism which manifests itself within the religious sentiment. This book had a considerable influence on artists of the time for whom it must have been a sort of breviary. Therefore, in the xivth century, the sensible interpretation of the Gospel seems to prevail. The renown of the great masters of the Trecento who become its servants, confers to it an authority which will allow it to counterbalance rapidly in all Europe the influence of the theological iconography proceeding from the ateliers of the French cathedrals.

Far from continuing this pathetic tradition of Italian iconography, Fra Angelico presents himself to us as radically reacting against it in the sense of operating a return to the theological spirit of the xiiith century. However, this does not mean that he did not exceptionally try his hand at the pathetic tradition as the celebrated *Descent from the Cross* of Santa Trinità attests (Pl. 89 to 93). But this picture, although an incomparable masterpiece from the plastic point of view, testifies that this domain was more or less foreign to Fra Angelico's serene soul. The forced expression he lends to his personages are painfully conceived by a peaceful man to whom passion and suffering are alike unknown. Yet this work was very celebrated in his time and one did not remark that it was to have an illustrious lineage. In the xivth century the different variants of the *Descent from the Cross* always showed the body of the Christ still holding to the cross by his feet and swaying towards the holy women, either bust forward or on his back. Most often only one ladder was placed against the cross, and the body was held back by only one personage. The pathos of these compositions resides in the brutal fall of the body which tips over, inert and dislocated. Fra Angelico innovates by showing the corpse entirely detached from the cross against the horizontal beams of which two ladders are placed. Joseph and Nicodemus hold the body which is moreover supported by John and an aid. Instead of falling brutally, the remains of Christ slip gently and almost vertically to the ground describing an harmonious arabesque which terminates in the gesture of the Magdalen kissing the feet of Jesus. The body preserves something of the majesty it had whilst on the cross. This composition which overthrows the traditional data of the theme, was much admired. The two ladders and the body entirely detached from the cross will be taken up again at the end of the century by Perugino and Signorelli. And the spirit of Fra Angelico's composition will even be transmitted through the intermediary of Daniel de Volterre to the celebrated works of Rubens and of Jouvenet.

The *frate's* soul is more accessible to tenderness than to pain. He therefore did not remain unacquainted with the sentiments of human affection which the Italian Middle-Ages lent to the group of the Virgin-Mother. If in his pictures the Virgin always preserves a certain gravity devoid of all severity, the pretty naked child sometimes clothed in an embroidered tunic such as that worn by the children of his time, plays with his mother, trying to seize the flower she offers him, or to hold a pomegranate in his hand, or even to bless, sometimes with the help of Mary. Repeating without almost any variant a composition by Don Lorenzo Monaco who himself had obtained it from the Sienese, Fra Angelico has depicted the Virgin who in a proud motherly gesture, presents Jesus, naked, who is thus offered very erect to the adoration of men (Pl. 58). Nor is he unaware of the coaxing gesture of the child caressing his mother's chin to " implore her not to cry any more ", according to the *Meditations* of the pseudo Bonaventura, a trait of tenderness which had obtained considerable success in the Marian iconography of the Middle-Ages (Pl. 56).

This human tendency is nevertheless exceptional in our painter. One could indeed divide his works into two parts — that which he accomplished for laymen or on the order of other monastic congregations, or that which he executed for his own Order at the Convent of St. Mark. There he worked for the spirituality of the Dominican Order with which his own was blended, for he was a perfect monk, having renounced all personal will. It is to St. Mark's that one should go to seek the deepest signification of his work. To the common people who came to pray in parish churches, Fra Angelico did not give the same images as those he reserved for the monks. To these the hymn of the creature, so apt to touch the humble, was not suitable. In order to exhort them to the orison which leads to contemplation, they required in their cells works which, as far as it was compatible with the very notion of art, were stripped of the creature and impressed with a deep theological signification. Thus it is that one sees every picturesque element disappear from the compositions at St. Mark's; the scenes or rather the visions are reduced to a few personages, or better still to a few religious figures which detach themselves against a plain background more suitable to the poverty of a mendicant order than the ancient golden Byzantine background, but also more abstract than the latter. Everything takes place out of time and space, in the eternity of the lithurgy. For the *frate*, the celebration of the Christian mysteries is not the commemoration of an historical event : it is actual, of the eternal actuality of revealed Truth of which it celebrates the different manifestations. Each of his compositions is an aspect of Christian Dogma plastically represented in the form of a symbol.

If one studies with care the iconography of the frescoes of St. Mark, one perceives that contrary to the traditions of the schools of Italian painting, Fra Angelico always chooses amongst the different themes proposed to him the theological version which he prefers to the pathetic version. Several examples show us this very clearly.

Bernardo Daddi. THE ANNUNCIATION. Musée du Louvre, Paris.

For the Sienese of the Trecento, the *Annunciation* had been an admirable dramatic motive. It gave them the opportunity of expressing that fateful instant when a human destiny orientates itself. Simone di Martino was the first to depict the panicky recoil of the frail young virgin before the sudden revelation of her dramatic destiny. Where is the human predestined to a certain happiness who would not draw back if, in his youth, he was told what it would cost him to live ? The tragic Barna da Siena took this attitude of fright up again. It was transmitted down to Don Lorenzo Monaco, a Florentine who owes so much to the Sienese (the *Annunciation* of the Academy of Florence). Another tradition of which Giotto was the initiator had won the favour of the Florentine school. It showed the Virgin submitting calmly to the sudden irruption of the divine and to the revelation of her destiny. One of the most beautiful illustrations of this theme is the small panel by Bernardo Daddi at the Louvre, in which the Virgin crosses her hands upon her bosom as if to contain the beating of her heart (fig. p. 33). It is this tradition more conformable to theology that Fra Angelico perpetuates. The pictures at Cortona and in the corridor of St. Mark are all conformable to Daddi's work (Pl. 69 and 174). In the cell of St. Mark, Fra Giovanni has accentuated still more the humble attitude of Mary; he represents her kneeling (Pl. 121). Indeed, contrary to Giotto who seems to believe that Mary's will drew its source from her own strength of soul, the Dominican painter insists upon the resignation of the Virgin's soul and her total abandonment to the Divine Will. He has loved this theme because it allowed him to express with a particular intensity that renunciation to all personal will which is demanded of the Christian soul. The Dominican order founded by a Canon of St. Augustine, had adopted this doctrine which had been applied for the first time by the Bishop of Hippone. St. Thomas Aquinas had also insisted upon this principle, and St. Teresa of Avila who, through the intermediary of the Dominicans, owes so much to augustinism, condensed it into one awful sentence which seems to deny free will to humans. It is this infusion of grace into a soul which has renounced all and thus utterly abandons itself to the divine motion, no longer outlining even the faintest protestation before the supreme will, that Fra Angelico expresses in his *Annunciations*. Renouncement being the monastic virtue *par excellence*, one can well understand how deep a signification this theme had for him. At the Convent of St. Mark the Annunciation which is at the top of the stairs leading to the first storey is like a warning given to the monks at that fearful hour when coming up from Complines, they regain for the rest of the night their cells in which they are about to find themselves once again, and during long hours, face to face with their own soul.

In the course of the xivth century a slow elaboration had transformed the Nativity, which at first had been conceived like a human event, into an adoration of the Child placed naked on the ground. At the beginning of the xvth century, this theme was almost formed. It is common in the work of Don Lorenzo Monaco and of Gentile da Fabiano. Fra Angelico takes it up again and completes it by making Joseph kneel. By converging the composition around the Child he expresses clearly this first act of the cult of latria (Pl. 168). The Nativity therefore becomes under his brush a symbol of the divinity of Jesus. There again we perceive the influence our painter may have had as a painter of images. The definitive form he has given to the Nativity will be adopted by the whole Quattrocento and Cinquecento. Besides the painters will not be attracted by the theological lesson but by the plastic qualities of the composition which is of a fine classical ordonnance.

If one recalls how without falling into the finicalness of the Trecentists and by preserving a natural dignity to the divine group, Fra Angelico had succeeded in expressing in his first images of the Madonna sentiments of human tenderness, — one is nevertheless struck by the austere figure which welcomes the visitor in the corridor of the first storey of the convent of St. Mark (Pl. 113). Mary graciously inclines her face towards the Child whom she contemplates with a pensive gravity. As for Him, he is no longer the smiling *Bambino* of the preceding Madonnas. He blesses with a truly sacerdotal solemnity. He has the same hieratic gesture and attitude as the children of the ancient Byzantine, romanesque, and " dugentesque " *theotocoi*. He even has the same costume. In fact he no longer wears the tunic of a *putto* of his time; he is garbed in the pallium of the philosophers of old which used to drape the Divine Children of antiquity (see fig. page 39). Thus the painter does not hesitate to abandon the human group and to revert to the old theological figure of the " Mother of God ", symbol of the Incarnation. The comparison of the face of this Madonna with that of another by Melchior di Jacopo, a painter of the Dugento (fig. page 37), suffices to show the perpetuity of Fra Angelico's Byzantine idealism.

But nothing is more remarkable at the Convent of St. Mark than the iconography of the Passion. The way in which the frescoist has interpreted the scenes of the Passion is so original with regard to his times that it deserves to be considered for a few moments.

The Primitive Church emerging from Paganism which had attributed so great a merit to the heroic cult of the human body, recoiled at imagining the sufferings of Christ. This sentiment had even given birth to a heresy, Docetism, professed by the monophysites who, denying the human nature of Christ, and recognizing only the divine, believed that the Passion was but an appearance. In spite of the condemnation Orthodoxy pronounced against this tendency, the iconography of the Passion remained wholly impregnated by it at Byzantium and in the Occident during the High Middle-Ages; this influence gave birth to the theme of the Triumphal Passion which in each of the scenes representing the Judgment and the Crucifixion made of Christ a voluntary victim, a hero who vanquished death. Thus the infamous punishment of the cross reserved to slaves was claimed by Christians as being the finest title of glory of the God made man. It became the very proof of the Christ's divinity resplendent under the outrage and physical misery. Whilst official iconography was becoming fixed at Byzantium, the Cappadocian monks who came from the people and who did not understand those theological subtilities, were elaborating a pathetic iconography of the Passion thus following the example of the Syrian monks. It is these images that the painters of the Dugento and of the Trecento, who for more than a century fixed the iconography of the Passion, sought as their models. The Christ will be painted by them like a prisoner of common law tortured, scoffed at, beaten, delivered up to the outrages of an undisciplined soldiery, suffering in his flesh and in his soul. No insult will be spared him; they will overlook no groan, no shiver of his wounded flesh, no spasm; they will show his quivering body caked in blood and twisted in agony on the cross. Once created, this iconography of the Passion will admit of no exception : one knows in what manner in the xvith century the German Grünewald reached the acme of sublime horror in the scene of the Crucifixion.

Studio of Fra Angelico. THE PLACING ON THE CROSS. Fresco.
Convent of San Marco, Florence. Cell 36.

In relation to the iconography practised in the School, the representation of the Passion which Fra Angelico painted at the Convent of St. Mark assumes a quite unusual character. In opposition to all tradition the dominican monk reverts to the triumphal and symbolic Passion of ancient ages. In the frescoes of St. Mark, the serenity of the Christ makes one think of the great theological cycles of Daphni, of St. Mark of Venice, and beyond them of St. Apollinarius of Ravenna, and of the Christian sarcophagi. The body of the crucified Christ which the Trecentists had shown racked and dislocated by the spasm of agony, holds itself on the cross in an attitude full of nobility; he is as smooth as an antique statue (Pl. 108). The impassibility of the face with its closed eyes makes one think of the impersonal figurations of death in classical Greek sculpture (Pl. 110). The various scenes of the Passion are stripped of every pathetic or picturesque episode which might present an historical import. In the Flagellation, the action is suppressed or rather symbolically

35

transferred to St. Dominic who is scourging himself as a self-inflicted discipline. It is the apologetic lesson which is stressed, not the subject itself. The cross which the Christ bears rests lightly upon his shoulder (fig. page 27) and no soldiers, no Jews escort him. Behind him walks Mary, " the compassionate ", who collaborates with her son in the work of Redemption. Making a gesture identical to that of Jesus, she follows him along the *via dolorosa*, and thus shows the way of salvation to the faithful, — which teaching is apparently understood by St. Thomas Aquinas who is kneeling. The three figures of this fresco resume in some sort the whole Christian dogma : the Incarnation, the Redemption, the Satisfaction — i.e. the collaboration which is demanded of the believer himself in working out his salvation.

In one of the artist's masterpieces the theological idea of the divinity of the Christ in the Passion is affirmed by a symbol to which the beauty of the composition confers a peculiar eloquence : it is the famous *Christ Crowned with Thorns* of the seventh cell (Pl. 117 and 119). This fresco seems to takes us back to the most distant ages before the reform accomplished by Giotto had introduced realism into art. The historical data of the scene is merely indicated by conventional signs in order that no realistic temptation should divert the interest from the symbolical meaning of the work (1). The most infamous scene of the Passion, that in which the dignity of the Christ was turned into derision, is transformed into a picture of majesty and power. Impassive under the outrage inflicted to him, Christ is truly King. One recalls that old Byzantine picture *The King of Glory*, which the realist westerners transformed into the Man of Sorrows. Imagination harks back to the XIth century, to that mosaic in St. Mark of Venice, in which the Christ, one size taller than his followers, wears his Crown of Thorns like a royal diadem which he claims proudly by the three words written on a phylactery : " *Spinis Coronatus Sum* ". Still further back in time, Memory evokes those Christian sarcophagi in which in lieu of a thorny headdress the Christ receives a crown of laurels like a hero of the stadium.

" *The King of Glory* " of the seventh cell has as companion another triumphant figure — the Christ of the *Transfiguration* in cell six (Pl. 116). It is not unintentionally that we have compared these two figures in the illustration of the present work. This scene appears very rarely in western iconography outside of illustrated books. Fra Angelico adopted it as being one of the symbolic figures testifying most clearly to the divinity of the Christ manifesting itself by means of a " theophany ". It is remarkable that he has represented it by following faithfully all the rules of Byzantine iconography : the latter ordered all the gestures and attitudes of the apostles which each had a determined symbolic signification.

Another subject, also rather rare in western iconography, and of which no other example exists in the Quattrocento, is the *Placing on the Cross*, of cell thirty-six, in which one sees the Christ extending his arms on the Cross and lending himself with docility to the will of the executioners (fig. page 35). Father Marchese and Gabriel Millet have both shown that this scene was the illustration of a passage from Isaiah which was commented in the XVIth century by the anonymous author of a legend of Mary-Magdalen : " *Oblatus est quia ipse voluit* ". This is the very sense of the triumphal Passion. The torture of the Cross is infamous only if submitted to. When voluntary, it becomes heroic.

The points of contact of Fra Angelico with Byzantine art are sometimes so direct that we are led to suppose that he must have perused, in some convent library, an old Greek manuscript containing those sacred images which were obsolete in his time. The following example strengthens this hypothesis.

There existed two variants of *Judas' Betrayal*. Giotto, who always inclined towards pathos, had followed the eastern theme which was more human and which opposed the traitor and the just man, Good and Evil, face to face. At Assisi, Cimabue, on the contrary, had preferred the Byzantine theme, showing Christ full face; in this divine fronting he does not take part in the action but remains insensible, as if absent to the insulting embrace. The artists of the Trecento had shared between themselves both variants, and had indeed disfigured the second by the dramatic accent they gave to it. Fra Angelico takes the Byzantine theme up again, and with such a great purity that it appears as directly related to Daphni and St.Mark of Venice, and beyond them to St. Apollinarius of Ravenna (fig. page 29).

---

(1) Don Lorenzo Monaco had already utilized these symbols of the Passion which, in the Middle Ages were called : "*Arma Christi*" (see fig. Page 40). But far from understanding their value as pure symbols, he had drawn a picturesque effect from them.

The affinity between Fra Angelico and Byzantine art is still more apparent in the way in which he represents the *Last Supper*. Caring little about the iconographic habits of the Occident, he depicts not the institution of the Eucharist according to the narrations of the Evangelists, but the Communion of the Apostles, under the form which the communion of the faithful assumes in Roman Catholic Lithurgy. How is it possible not to recall that sublime scene called *The Divine Lithurgy* which the Byzantines were wont to represent in the curves of the apses above the altar, and which possesses such a high symbolic signification? This representation, which we see for the first time on Syrian lithurgic silverware of the vith century, decorated perhaps the apse of the celebrated church of the Holy Apostles which Justinian erected at Constantinople. It also occupied the apse of St. Sophia of Kiev, and of Serrès, in Macedonia, in the xith century. It was next found in the rupestrine churches of Cappadoccia, and later in Macedonian art of the xivth century; and lastly in Servian churches. In the Occident, the xiiith century Psalter of Ingeburge depicts the Last Supper in the same manner; but this example was seldom followed. Jean Fouquet's composition in the Hours of Etienne Chevalier draws its inspiration from another direction; none comes as close to the Greek theme as that of Fra Angelico; one may conjecture that the picture painted in 1488 for the Corpus Christi Confraternity of Urbino by Justus of Ghent was inspired by that of the *frate*. The latter surpasses even

Megliore di Jacopo. THE VIRGIN AND CHILD. Detail.
Stoclet Collection, Brussels (cf. plate 114).

the Byzantines by the liturgical actuality he lends to the *Last Supper*. Scorning the Gospel narrations, he causes the Virgin to take part in it. He transforms the guest chamber into a monastic refectory the rustic furnishings of which evoke the simplicity of the early Franciscan and Dominican ages, and where the apostles, assembled around the bare table, receive from the Christ the celestial food just like the Dominican monks of the predella at the Louvre who are also seated before an empty table awaiting that the angels should give them their provender (fig. page 43).

If one wished to lay down the principles of a spirituality peculiar to Fra Angelico, as one has done for those saints who fixed their mystical states in writing, one would be justified to say that one of the most singular traits of the *frate's* mysticism is his devotion to the Dogma of the Communion of Saints. In all the scenes painted in the convent of St. Mark, saints of both sexes participate in the act which indeed consists wholly in adoration and prayer.

It was this devotion, as much as his plastic instinct, which led Fra Angelico to constitute the definitive form of the theme of the *Sacra Conversazione* which unites the Virgin, the Child and the Elect in an eternal colloquy. The great *Maestes* by Duccio, Simone di Martino, and Lippo Memmi already contained this theme in all its amplitude; they depicted the angels and the saints grouped around the Madonna and united in a concert of praise. The *Sacra Conversazione* might have sprung from examples such as these; but a whole century, and the genius of Fra Giovanni, were needed for that lesson to bear its fruits. During all the xivth century and even during the first part of the xvth, in schools of secondary importance, Saints continued to align themselves in hieratic and isolated order around a central figure or scene in which they took no part.

If it happens that they sometimes group themselves around Mary's throne in a same panel, they are hardly less stiff and no spiritual link unites them. Fra Angelico himself has been guilty of this inexpressive juxtaposition of holy personages (Pl. 68). What a difference with the magnificent *Te Deum* which the high altar of St. Mark is (Pl. 138) !

The idea of grouping the saints around the Crucifix is not Fra Angelico's own. In the course of the XIVth century one sees a saint or two appear here and there in a Crucifixion. A fresco of the Collegio di Napoli at Assisi which is due to a direct disciple of Giotto's, shows, grouped around the crucified Christ, several saints who all make the same symmetrical gesture in order to express their sorrow. The work possesses an indisputable decorative grandeur, and Fra Angelico who certainly made pilgrimages to Assisi when he was at Cortona, was able to see it and to retain the idea. But it is a far cry from monotonous repetition of the same gesture to the living variety of attitudes and expressions by which, in the great fresco of the chapter of St. Mark (Pl. 126 to 131), each saint exteriorizes according to his character the intimate reaction which the contemplation of the mystery of the death of Christ produces in his soul. This is indeed what Pér400 té calls very justly " a holy conversation at the foot of the Cross ". This work, in which the chief spiritual leaders of the Church Doctors and Founders of Orders are seen meditating before the mystery of the Christian Religion, is one of the most remarkable expressions of that Communion of Saints to which Fra Angelico appeared to attach so high a meaning in spiritual life. Is not the Communion of Saints an essentially monastic devotion ? For the monk cloistered in his convent are not the inhabitants of heaven more living and more actual than those of the earth ?

Whilst studying Fra Angelico we should constantly bear in mind that he did not belong to the category of lay brothers to which artist-monks generally pertained, but to that of father of the choir. He even became the prior of the convent of Fiesole. He had therefore received a very sound theological formation, and it would be rather surprising if no reflection of it were to be found in his art.

Thus by the high dogmatic signification it assumes, by its withdrawal from passion, and by its abstraction, the *frate's* work and especially at the convent of St. Mark, resumes direct contact with the traditions of the sacred art of the French XIIIth century extinct since more than a hundred years. We have seen that it often even plunges its roots deep into Byzantine art. One may ask oneself if this persistance should not be explained by the spirit of the Order to which the artist belonged ? Although they exerted upon art a far less deep impression than the Franciscans, the Dominicans had none the less their own aesthetic traditions. Indirectly through the preponderance they enjoyed at the University of Paris they no doubt contributed to the expansion of the dogmatic art of the French XIIIth century. The frescoes of the Chapel of the Spaniards of the Convent of Santa Maria Novella of Florence, that were painted on their order by Andrea da Firenze, constitute one of the most scholastic ensembles of the Middle-Ages. It is not surprising to discover this dogmatic spirit anew in the work of Fra Angelico, a reformed Dominican of the Congregation of the Observance, which practised the return to a strict application of the primitive Dominican rule and spirit.

One has therefore some difficulty in understanding Muratoff's assertion denying all dogmatic intention to Fra Angelico. According to him, that painter was " one of the most zealous destructors of the old traditions of Christian iconography which Byzantine painting had so jealously preserved ". An exact study of a few themes had proved us, on the contrary, that Fra Angelico respected the oldest iconographic traditions with a fervour absolutely unique in his time.

Muratoff's reaction, like that of Van Marle, can no doubt be explained by the irritation which so many theological and mystical speculations devoid of foundation and due to pious writers produce in these historians. But to make of Fra Angelico a pure plastician in the manner of Masaccio, is an excess at least as blameworthy as to make of him a monk who, confined in his cell, translated in painting the visions he might have been favoured with in moments of ecstasy. It would be surprising that this artist who was brought up in the Dominican order of which he practised the observance to the degree of holiness, did not know and practise the pure traditional doctrine according to which Art was at the service of Dogma. The whole of the Middle-Ages lived on this article of the Seventh Council of Nicea : " Art alone belongs to the painter. The Ordonnance and disposition belong to the Fathers ". Strictly applied to the XIIIth century, this division of a work of art into conception and execution found itself from the XIVth century onwards overrun by the manifestations of popular piety which introduced so many perceptible and anecdotal elements into iconography.

In the case of the panels of the convent of St. Mark, the ancient Byzantine conception which places Form under the domination of the Idea lives once more in all its purity. The artist is submissive to the theologian; but the one and the other are united in one and the same person, — the person of a saint.

Is it not surprising, and in a certain way paradoxical that this high expression of Christian thought should manifest itself at the very moment when the latter is about to cease communicating its inspiration to Art? Is it not strange that that sublime expression of the Middle-Ages should flourish precisely when the latter is entering into its decline?

This curious phenomenon corresponds with others of the same order which Mr. Huizinga has analysed in his book on the " Decline of the Middle-Ages " — one of the most penetrating works ever written on that complex epoch, the xvth century. Mr. Huizinga has shown that the declining Middle-Ages experienced a recrudescence of all the Ideals which had motivated its aspirations : knighthood, courtesy, religion. At the moment when they are about to cease to determine the creative activity of men, the values of civilization

Margaritone d'Arezzo. THE VIRGIN AND CHILD. Detail.
Phillip Lehman Collection, New York (cf. plate 115).

which the Middle-Ages had generated become more subtle, and assume in the thought of contemporaries a character both ethereal and sublime. In the first half of the xvth century, there took place a real crisis of " unrealism " of which Mr. Henri Focillon has noted the artistic effects in his book " *Art d'Occident* ". Imaginations delight in chivalrous, hagiographical, and courteous legends which flourish in the pages of manuscripts illustrated by the Limbourg brothers, and in Pisanello's frescoes. Art no longer translates thoughts or dogmas but dreams. In the religious domain this phenomenon produces an etherealized art which seems a contemplative vision of Paradise. Pictures are filled with angels, virgins, immaterial beings, pure spirits. A real craze for angels takes possession of the painters. The xvth century is truly the century of angels. Their graceful light swarms people the covings of cathedrals, the pages of manuscripts, the space of painted panels.

The Rhenish school has expressed this mystical idyllism with a particular suavity, — bringing to it that profound instinct of unrealism which is essential to the German soul. Fra Angelico takes part in this movement which affects all the countries of Europe; he is the spiritual brother of the Westphalian and Czech painters whose ecstatic visions paint celestial meadows peopled with Madonnas, birds, angels, and virgins. Thus the very sublimity of his art is not the expression of an apex, but of a decline.

Simultaneously with a renewal of idealism, one notices in the Europe of the first half of the xvth century a progression of naturalism. These two tendencies far from being contradictory blend perfectly with each other. The artist directs his gaze towards nature but, like St. Francis of Assisi, it is to celebrate its beauty and not to discover its truth. The positivist generation which will dissect realism almost cruelly is preceded by another that transfers to nature the mystical spirit it still retains from the Middle-Ages. In all the religious paintings of this epoch, the artist has no longer recourse to the symbol. Characteristic from this point of view is the immense theological ensemble of the *Mystic Lamb* of Ghent, in which the whole dogma is expressed under perfectly real appearances and by means of images borrowed from normal life. Fra Angelico proceeds in the same way; he makes use of the discoveries of his time on Space and Volume so as to give an appearance of reality to his personages. Like Van Eyck, like the Rhenish painters of the same epoch, he represents Paradise not by allegories and symbols, but by means of a spring meadow bestrewed with flowerets, i.e. under a natural form. Thus in this first stage of naturalism the artist, although still imbued with the spirit of the Middle-Ages, remains dominated by spiritualistic aims; but he expresses the supernatural by giving it the appearance of the real world. Before being studied and loved for itself Nature attracts man as an image of the Creator's beauty. This " mystical naturalism " is the last manifestation and the apotheosis of the Franciscan spirit in Art. Fra Angelico is its highest expression.

Don Lorenzo Monaco. CHRIST OF PITY.
The Academy, Florence.

THE MASTER-WORKMAN

UNTIL modern times all the production of painting was achieved by collective execution. Michael-Angelo chasing his aids from the Sixtine Chapel in order to remain face to face with his huge work, inaugurated the stern individualism of the modern age by which art becomes a romantic confession. Collective work appeared all the more normal to Italians that their intellective tendencies inclined them to situate invention in the conception of a work, the execution of the latter being considered by them as a material operation of secondary importance; Leonardo da Vinci will clearly separate the two operations and apply this division of the task by having most of his works painted by his pupils. One hardly imagines a Van Eyck acting thus, as for Northern artists painting confounds itself with the material action which gives it life. Since Giotto the great decorative cycles were executed by the pupils of the *bottega*, under the direction of the master, who reserved himself the invention of the cartoons, and the execution of the most noble parts of the painting. Raphael himself will not proceed otherwise; he will even push this process so far as to become a sort of master-workman exercising a high direction over the enterprise with the aid of an overseer named Jules Romains in whom he had full confidence. The principles of classicism which establish the beauty of a work of art on an ensemble of rationally conceived and intellectually transmissible norms, quite naturally favoured this tendency. The conceptions of the Middle-Ages also lent themselves to it, art being in fact before all illustration, the translation of ideas into forms. What was primordial was the iconographic composition which had to be clear and expressive, and which the master could entrust to no one; the more or less skilful way in which the execution was carried out was of much less consequence. In a collective cycle like that of Giotto, at St. Francis of Assisi, his contemporaries were no doubt less expert than we are in distinguishing the different hands.

However one notices in the Quattrocento a withdrawal from this collective spirit in favour of individualism. The artists belonging to the generation of pioneers, such as Masaccio, Paolo Ucello, Andrea del Castagno, Alessio Baldovinetti, seem to have depended a great deal less on the assistance of an atelier than their forerunners; moreover, their work is limited. With them art ceases to be imagery-making and becomes a plastic problem, the novelty of which requires the whole effort of the artist. A Florentine artist of the Quattrocento has however preserved the collective methods of the past, and has even enlarged them : this is Fra Angelico. As early as 1907, Aloïs Wurm drew attention upon the unequalness of the work attributed to this painter to whom, in an access of excessive severity, he only conceded a few of the frescoes of St. Mark, and, here and there, a few personages in the altar-pieces. In the chapter devoted to Fra Angelico in Vol. X of *The Italian Schools of Painting*, which appeared in 1928, Raymond Van Marle tried to make a classification of the authentic and the apocryphal works, which was taken up again with certain variants by Paul Muratoff. The existence of numerous apocryphal works and the extensive foreign collaboration in the works traditionally attributed to Fra Angelico, are no longer contested. Most of these statements have been approved by the catalogue of the Museum of St. Mark. It is therefore greatly surprising to see a recent monography, that of Mr. Edouard Schneider, mingle indiscriminately the authentic works and the others as if the problem did not exist.

The inequality in the *frate's* work renders its study particularly irritating for whoever undertakes it; for the artist had assistants of such talent that it is not always easy to determine whether one is really in presence of a personal work, or of one executed by a pupil. The best rule is to discard any work about which one entertains the slightest doubt. The paintings which are indisputably and entirely by the hand of Fra Angelico, such as the *Annunciation* of Cortona, shine with such a splendour of perfection in their execution that a certain laxity can only be explained as being due to an aid. Nor can one attribute to a period of formation, as one might be tempted to do, some pictures sill very near to illuminations (such as the famous *Last Judgment* of the Museum of St. Mark) which present certain weaknesses of execution. The reliquary of *Santa Maria Novella*, bearing the *Annunciation* and the *Adoration of the Magi*, proves indeed that Fra Angelico reached that perfection of execution in his very first works. It also attests that he employed the method of collective work quite early in his career as painter, for this panel forms part of an ensemble of four reliquaries painted for Santa Maria Novella, of which only two are probably by him — i.e. the one above mentioned, and the *Madonna of the Star* (Pl. 56). In spite of Van Marle's opinion, this latter work must be attributed to him with the exception perhaps of the angels, the damaged state of the painting sufficing to explain a certain inferiority in comparison with the first reliquary (Pl. 53 and 54). Indeed in any judgment one may pass on a work by Fra Angelico, one should always take into account its state of preservation; that is why it is reasonable to beware of an examination made only from reproductions, more especially as Italian photographic publishers have the habit of retouching unashamedly their documents in order to give them an academic aspect which pleases the inhabitants of the peninsula. We have therefore thought preferable in this work to pronounce ourselves only after having carefully studied the originals, whilst believing that in the face of such delicate problems it was best to incline towards severity than towards indulgence.

In the important painted work connected with the name of Fra Angelico, there exists a decreasing scale of authenticity from the original works to the productions of pupils who imitated the master. Rare are the paintings entirely by his own hand. Many were executed by him in collaboration with one or several aids. Others, which are attributed in this book to his " atelier ", are due entirely to aids, but were executed after a cartoon by the master of the *bottega* and under his attentive supervision. We have considered these as belonging to him at least by the conception. Amongst these are some true masterpieces worthy of the master. We reserve the attribution of " school " to all the works executed in Fra Angelico's sphere but not under his direct inspiration.

In order to discern better the different manners which are concealed for the public at large under the name of Fra Angelico, one should establish a distinction according to techniques for with rare exceptions the aids of his atelier seem to have been specialized in fresco-painting, in illuminating, and in painting on panels.

The study of the decoration of the Convent of St. Mark makes it relatively easy to distribute the frescoes between the painter and his atelier. All the frescoes situated around the cloister of St. Antoninus are by his own hand. The large *Crucifixion* of the chapter which has been rather too harshly treated by some authors, shows certain inequalities. The ensemble of the saints on the right hand side is one of the artist's finest creations, whereas the group of the Virgin supported by the holy women is by an aid whom we propose to call " the Master of the Nativity ". He is by far the most productive pupil of the atelier. But the execution of the medaillons is very inferior and is due to an extremely indifferent painter.

In the decoration of the first storey a severe criticism must only retain seven frescoes in which the personal manner of Fra Angelico shines in all its splendour. These are on the one hand the *Crucifixion* (Pl. 131) and the *Holy Conversation* of the corridor (Pl. 109, 113 and 115), both of which were painted with the help of aids, and on the other hand the frescoes of the cells which skirt the Via Lamarmora i.e. the *Annunciation* (Pl. 121, 122, 123), — the *Transfiguration* (Pl. 116, 118), — the *Christ Mocked* (Pl. 117, 119, 120), — the *Coronation of the Virgin* (Pl. 124), and the *Presentation at the Temple* (Pl. 112).

Van Marle has shown a rather excessive generosity in the separation he has made between the original frescoes and the others, for he retains works which rightfully should be discarded such as the celebrated

Annunciation in the corridor.   But no classification has been attempted between the numerous frescoes due to the master's assistants except in the case of those which Mr. Paolo d'Ancona attributes to Bernardo Strozzi, — which attribution cannot be retained for reasons we will expose further on.   It is not impossible, however, to discern distinct manners in this series; two groups at least detach themselves rather plainly from the ensemble.

The assistant who painted the *Nativity* of cell five (Pl. 168), that composition in which the distribution of the figures in space is so characteristic of the *frate's* art, was one of the disciples who best imbued himself with his master's spirit, although with certain archaïsms.   By his angular style, his elongated proportions, his stiff draperies, he remains a belated Gothic; he does not know well how to situate bodies in space; the

Studio of Fra Angelico.   THE INSTITUTION OF THE EUCHARIST.   Fresco.
Convent of San Marco, Florence.   Cell 35.

wrinkled faces of his personages with their long noses and their slanting eyes, still retain something of the grimace peculiar to Giotto's school.   His hands are often rather clumsy at the articulations (Pl. 171).   This artist is responsible for some of the best frescoes of the convent : the *Threnody* of cell two (Pl. 169), the *Christ on the Mount of Olives* of cell thirty-four (Pl. 170); *The Virgin between Two Saints* of cell eleven; his hand is also recognizable in the Virgin of the *Christ Mocked* (Pl. 171), and in the two groups of Saints of the *Madonna* of the corridor (Pl. 109), and perhaps also in *The Last Supper* of cell twenty-six (fig. page 43).   This assistant's collaboration does not extend only to the frescoes, but also to panels.   One recognizes his manner in the left part of the *Descent from the Cross* of Santa Trinità (Pl. 89).   It is even possible to attribute to him the whole execution of the *Threnody*, in distemper, of the Museum of St. Mark (Pl. 172).   The archaïc draperies, the face of the long-nosed Virgin, the inability of the artist to make the volumes " turn ", a certain tendency towards asceticism, and a great understanding of the distribution of the figures in space, all these characteristics tend to point to the Master of Nativity as the author of this work.

Two celebrated compositions which one does not resign oneself easily to withdraw from the personal work of the artist, the *Annunciation* of the Corridor (Pl. 174) a very celebrated painting, and the *Noli me Tangere* of cell one (Pl. 141), should be restored to the best of all Fra Angelico's assistants.   This pupil, whom one might surname the " Master of the Annunciation ", has succeeded in making the *frate's* manner his own with a remarkable ease but not without a certain " stylization " which allows one to detect him.   This stylization is particularly obvious in his profiles in which he indeed reproduces the linear arabesques of Fra Angelico, but with something rather more dry and more scrupulously accurate.   The grouping of the heads allows one to notice the remarkable continuity of this characteristic in this painter.   He distinguishes himself among all the other aids of the atelier by the skill with which he draws hands; yet these are always a little shorter than those drawn by his master.   He also is less skilful in making volumes " turn ", as is shown by the slightly flattened face of the Virgin in the *Annunciation*.   To this artist one can attribute, with certitude besides the *Annunciation* and the *Noli me Tangere*, the *Adoration of the Magi* of the cell of Cosimo de' Medici (Pl. 175).   In the great *Crucifix* of the corridor, at the foot of which St. Dominic is seen praying (Pl. 126), I believe the figure of the Saint to be by the Master of the Annunciation even if the Christ is surely due to the brush of Fra Angelico.

The two masters we have just defined may have worked in common.   The *Resurrection* of cell eight (Pl. 176) seems indeed the product of their collaboration.   One recognizes the style of the Master of the Annunciation in the beautiful Angel seated on the sepulchre, whilst the manner of the Master of the Nativity is apparent in the group of holy women, with their elongated proportions and gothic draperies.

Among the other frescoes it is difficult to distinguish personal manners except, perrhaps, degrees of values.   They are the anonymous production of the atelier.   They possess few peculiar characteristics, but present only a more or less great decline of the art of the master-workman.   The *Descent to the Limbos* (cell thirty-one), the *Bearing of the Cross* (cell twenty eight, page 27), the *Sermon on the Mount* (cell thirty two), the *Betraval of Judas* (cell thirty three, page 25), all seem to be by the same hand.   Certain works must have been executed after Fra Angelico's departure according to his suggestions but far from his personal impulsion. He had perhaps entrusted the direction of his atelier to the Master of the Nativity, for here and there one seems to catch a glimpse of the latter's spirit though rather diluted and degenerated.   It was certainly far from the frate's influence, and perhaps even after his death, that the decoration of the convent was hastily completed. The lack of invention is proven by the way in which was painted uniformly a whole series of very indifferent crucifixions which decorate cells fifteen to twenty-three, and cells twenty-nine, thirty, forty, and forty-one.

Perhaps this important collective participation in the frescoes of the convent of St. Mark can be explained by the fact that Fra Angelico occupied the office of Father of the Choir, which obliged him to attend the regular church services, and forced him to entrust to lay brothers the material execution of a great part of his work.   In any case if, at the epoch of his maturity, he made use of so extensive a collaboration, he was to do so with still more reason in the works of his old age.   The Frescoes left unfinished at Orvieto as well as those of the Vatican, indicate indeed so great a concourse of pupils that it is often difficult to discern in them the touch of the Master.   It is true that the four successive restorations to which the unfortunate works of the Vatican have been subjected should incline one to prudence in judging their quality.   The names of the pupils who helped the *frate* in the Chapel of the Holy Sacrament, and at Orvieto, are known to us : amongst them only one, Benozzo Gozzoli, will achieve a career in the history of Italian painting.   If no document has revealed us the names of the aids who collaborated to the " studio " of Nicholas V, one can at least affirm with certitude that Gozzoli played an important part in it.   Carried away by the affinities of style which the latter's work presents with the Vatican frescoes, certain historians, such as Van Marle and Muratoff, are prone to attribute him too great a personal influence on the destinies of Fra Angelico's art. Does not Van Marle even go as far as to consider that the whole of the *Life of St. Stephen* is by the hand of Gozzoli ?   According to these authors one would imagine Fra Angelico as a weak old man, whose trembling hand was supported by young Benozzo.   It is far more natural to believe that Fra Angelico is himself responsible for the transformation of style one notices at Orvieto and at Rome, and that Benozzo drew from it the source of his own style.   Indeed Gozzoli's first personal works at Montefalco and at San Gemignano are far from attaining the undeniable amplitude of the compositions, and the majesty of the figures of the Vatican frescoes.   In all his works, even in the best, such as those of the Chapel of the Riccardi palace in Florence, and those of the Campo Santo of Pisa, Benozzo Gozzoli appears as an inferior disciple of the author of the " studio " of Nicholas V.

One can presume that Gozzoli played in the atelier of Rome a part analogous to that which seems to have been attributed at St. Mark to the anonymous artist we have called the Master of the Nativity, that is to say a function of overseer similar to that held later by Jules Romains in Raphael's studio.   If the compositions executed by this means have not the same perfection as those of St. Mark, it is due to a slackening in Fra Angelico's own style at that epoch, and perhaps also to the fact that being older he no longer supervised as carefully as of yore the material execution of the frescoes.

Far from astonishing one, the inequality of the Vatican frescoes should therefore appear as normal since one discovers it in all the works our artist has produced. The *Story of St. Lawrence* (Pl. 146, 147, 148, 150, 156) is incontestably superior to that of St. Stephen (Pl. 151, 152, 153); the rhythms of the compositions are superior, and the personages are better constructed. Perhaps the *Legend of St. Lawrence* was the first executed. Contrarily to the opinions of Van Marle and of Muratoff, the four evangelists of the ceiling (Pl. 144 and 145) appear to me to be of a fine inspiration and emanating directly from the master. On the other hand six Doctors and Fathers of the Church standing under the Gothic dais decorating the arches of the chapel, bear the mark of Benozzo's heavy art and loose style. As for the St. Bonaventura and St. Thomas Aquinas they are indisputably two masterpieces.

As Van Marle has remarked, the degeneracy of the style of the Vatican frescoes gave rise to the Umbrian style of the second half of the xvth century, the most symptomatic representatives of which are such decorators as Bonfigli and Caporali. It would seem as it Gozzoli had transmitted this style to the Umbrians.

With the establishment of the Convent of St. Mark corresponded the constitution of a library due to the liberalities of Cosimo de' Medici. A regular school of miniaturists worked at the decoration of the lithurgical books. These books were formerly attributed to Fra Angelico himself and later to his brother Benedetto da Mugello, who entered the Fiesole convent at the same time as him and who, according to tradition, was a miniaturist. But recent documents have proved that Benedetto was only a copyist and a calligrapher. Mr. Paolo d'Ancona has the merit of having thrown some light upon the school of illumination at St. Mark's; one also owes him a monumental work on Florentine miniature. He showed that most of the manuscripts produced by this school were the works of Zanobi Strozzi (1412-1468), a member of the illustrious Florentine family; from 1446 to 1453 he worked for Cosimo de' Medici at illustrating the great antiphonaries of St. Mark with the collaboration of Filippo di Matteo Torelli for the ornementation. This Zanobi Strozzi whom Vasari mentions amongst the pupils of Fra Angelico, must have been Director of the atelier of the Book-department at St. Mark's transforming into illuminations the compositions and the iconographic themes of his master. The school of the miniaturists of St. Mark creditably continues that of the Convent of Camaldolite monks founded by Don Lorenzo Monaco. It produced the last fine works of this art which had never been greatly developed in Florence (Pl. 157). Whereas in France, the art of the miniature has been secularized for two centuries, in Florence it still remains in the xvth century a monastic art as in the Romanesque period.

A close study of the Convent of St. Mark has shown how extensive could be the collaboration to which Fra Angelico had recourse to second him with his monumental undertakings. This proceeding is not surprising in the case of fresco painting, as the material conditions of execution made team-work necessary. It astonishes more in the case of distempering. One can say that there is hardly a panel which was executed entirely by the hand of Fra Angelico. Sometimes he distributes parts of the work among several aids. He proceeded thus in the case of the celebrated *Madonna* of the Linaiuoli (Pl. 78) in which only the Virgin and the Angels are by his own hand. The side panels were painted by an aid who was more subjected than his master to the influence of Masaccio, whilst the predella was executed by another. In the altar screen of Perugia (Pl. 84), the St. John and the St. Catherine of the right panel contrast greatly, with their loose drawing, with St. Dominic and St. Nicholas of the left panel which are by Fra Angelico himself like the Madonna and the Angels of the center panel. At other times, the hands of both master and pupils blend in the ensemble of a work as in the *Coronation of the Virgin*, of the Museum of St. Mark (Pl. 61, 64 to 66). Even in the *Coronation* which is at the Louvre, and which is one of the most purely authentic works of Fra Angelico, a foreign intervention can be noticed here and there in a few of the heads. On the contrary, the *Annunciation* of Cortona is undoubtedly by his own hand and that is why it shines in his whole work with an incomparable brillance. Alone the two last panels of the predella are by his pupils.

The predella is the part of the work which Fra Angelico abandoned most willingly to the care of his pupils. The only predellas which are indisputably by his hand are those of the *Annunciation* (Pl. 85, 94, 95) of Cortona (with the above mentioned reservation), that of the *Coronation of the Virgin* at the Louvre (Pl. 96 to 103) except perhaps the last panel, and that, dispersed among many museums, which represents the *Legends of St. Cosmas and St. Damian* (Pl. 132 to 137). The severity manifested by certain authors in regard to this last-named work can only be explained by the bad state of preservation of certain of these panels. I fail to understand that Muratoff who generally has such a sound critical judgment, should prefer to this work the other predella of the same legend which can be found at St. Mark's, — a coarse work which is very alien to Fra Angelico both in conception and in execution. The rapprochement made here of certain panels treating of the same subject and which belong to the two ensembles (Pl. 136 and 137), show the difference in the quality of each.

If it is comparatively easy to distinguish the personalities of the different aids in the whole of the frescoes of St. Mark, this task is far more difficult in the case of tempera paintings. Starting from the miniatures of Bernardo Strozzi revealed by Mr. Paolo d'Ancona, Messrs. Berenson and Van Marle have attributed to this master a certain number of painted panels, and in particular the celebrated *Last Judgment* of the Camaldolites (Pl. 160-161), one of the most popular works to which the name of Fra Angelico is attached. But this group is very heterogenous. How is it possible to believe that works presenting such divergent compositions as the above-mentioned picture, the predella of the *Last Judgment* of the National Gallery, that of the *Linaiuoli*, that of the *Legends of St. Cosmas and St. Damian* of the Museum of St. Mark, the *Zaccharias Writing the Name of John* of the same museum, could be by the same hand without counting the collaboration which Van Marle attributes to Strozzi in the *Coronation of the Virgin* of the Museum of St. Mark, and in the *sportelli* of the Annunziata. As for the frescoes in cells thirty-one to thirty-five in St. Mark's convent, I own that the similitude suggested by Mr. Paolo d'Ancona between these and the miniatures of the convent does not appear to me to go further than those analogies of style contained in all that is connected with the art of Fra Angelico.

A comparative study of the miniatures and of the panels made at St. Mark's has not convinced me of the exactitude of these attributions. One can discern several hands in the miniatures ordered of Bernardo Strozzi. The manners of two artists can be recognized with a certain constancy; the one proceeds by lines, the illuminator draws the contours with precision by means of a fine, sharp stroke, and blends the touches under a uniform modelling; the other makes use of far more brush work; the latter artist has also a tendency to scamp the modelling and to leave the touches apparent. It is impossible to know which of these two manners belonged to Bernardo Strozzi himself. The first, which is that of a patient illuminator, is noticeable in the predella of the *Linaiuoli* (Pl. 165, 166, 167), — in the *Zaccharias Writing the Name of John* (Pl. 149), in the *Marriage and Death of the Virgin* of St. Mark's Museum, — three works which are certainly by the same hand. The hasty manner appears in the *Last Judgment* of the Camaldolites, and in the *sportelli* of the Annunziata, and particularly in the panels of the *Last Supper*, the *Betrayal of Judas*, the *Agony in the Garden*, the *Christ Mocked*, and the *Flagellation*.

The ingenuous perspicacity of Mr. Berenson has grouped around the same personality a certain number of " school " paintings presenting common characteristics, and which comprise, notably, a *Madonna* of the Museum of St. Mark, and the *Annunciation* of the National Gallery. The historian Van Marle has taken this grouping up again and has enlarged it perhaps rather improperly. The group constituted by Mr. Berenson appears coherent; nevertheless, it does not seem as if one could connect it with the name of Domenico di Michelino whom Vasari describes as having been one of Fra Angelico's pupils, and who lived from 1417 to 1491. The only authentic work one knows of this artist, the portrait of Dante with the symbol of the Divine Comedy, is placed so high up in the Dome of Florence, that it is hardly possible to draw from it sufficient and precise deductions as to the style and character of this painter.

The cupboard panels of the Annunziata seem to us a vast atelier work to which Fra Angelico contributed only general directions. Although they have made a choice between these works, Messrs. Berenson and Van Marle have shown them an excessive indulgence. Being rather inclined to consider Fra Angelico as a belated Gothic, they have not been struck by the archaïc character of these works in comparison with the preceding and contemporary creations of the artist. I prefer the severe opinion of Mr. Muratoff for whom these pictures are not directly due to the art of the painter of Fiesole and who sees in them no sign of his hand. One should indeed remember that at the moment these *sportelli* were ordered, i.e. towards 1448, Fra Angelico was in Rome. As he was elected prior of the Fiesole convent in 1449, one can also deduce that these new functions prevented him from working at this ensemble. The first panel which bears the *Annunciation* (Pl. 174), — the *Adoration of the Magi*, — the *Nativity*, — the *Flight into Egypt* (Pl. 173, 177, 178), — the *Presentation in the Temple*, — and *Ezekiel's Wheel*, is the only one which received the direct impulse of the master. *The Flight into Egypt* is so full of charm that many readers will be surprised at seeing it figure here among the works of his atelier. One hesitates, indeed, to deny to Fra Angelico the tender figure of this

Virgin, one of the most poetic among all those included in marian iconography. And yet this charming panel is typically a " school " work. It therefore deserves that one should consider it for a moment. It is not only the absence of style in Joseph's figure, nor the heavy drawing of the donkey that prevent one from attributing it to Fra Angelico himself, but also the spirit of the composition. If the landscape (Pl. 173) evokes by its beauty that of the *Martyrdom of St. Cosmas and St. Damian* of the Louvre (Pl. 132), the comparison between the two pictures illustrates well that which distinguishes a work of genius from that of a gifted pupil. *The Flight into Egypt* does not possess that cadence in the composition, that exactness of proportion between the landscape and the personages which make the beauty of the *Martyrdom*. There exists no link between the scene and the natural surroundings. The artist has preserved those medieval prejudices which considered the landscape merely as an necessary element; he still makes use of the old processes of the Giotto school inherited from Byzantium, and which consist in propping up the personages in bas-relief by modelling into their silhouette the outlines of certain planes of scenery; thus the geometrical projections of the figure of St. Joseph and of the group of the Virgin and the donkey appear in the outlines of the rocks against which they stand out; these form a wall which separates the figures hermetically from the landscape. There are, in a way, two pictures in one. The charming landscape itself with its dead trees, its cottage and haystack, possesses a picturesque accent nearer to Sasseta than to Fra Angelico, and very different from the noble architectonic abstraction of the *Martyrdom*. The vision of the painter of genius to whom one owes the *Martyrdom*, is a new vision liberated from traditions and which creates the plastic elements anew, starting from a direct observation of nature; in the author of the *Flight into Egypt*, a pictural subject immediately provokes mental automatisms. His imagination provides him with recipes but does not orientate him towards inventions. By a subtle symbiosis which makes the case of Fra Angelico one which is almost unique in the history of painting, he has known how to assimilate the poetry of his master's art, but has not understood its plastic spirit.

The three other panels of the cupboard are studio variants of iconographic compositions by the Blessed One. Most of these works betray an imitation of the Florentine style and yet in a few panels such as the *Washing of Feet*, the *Massacre of the Innocents*, the *Communion of the Apostles*, the *Presentation at the Temple*, the apparition of architectures *à la romaine* prove that Fra Angelico had not lost all contact with the atelier which had undertaken this work. One recognizes in the *Washing of Feet* (Pl. 179), an antique peristyle similar to those which were later to be exhumated at Pompeï and which also appears in one of the frescoes of the " studio " of Nicholas V (Pl. 148). One can distinguish the work of many different hands in this ensemble, and in particular those of the above mentioned miniaturists. The *Massacre of the Innocents* certainly appears to have been painted by the author of the predella of the Linaiuoli. Alessio Baldovinetti who, as Vasari has informed us, was one of Fra Angelico's pupils, certainly executed the *Marriage of Cana*, the *Baptism of Christ*, and the *Transfiguration ;* Baldovinetti's rugged style, after the manner of Castagno, contrasts strangely with the angelic sweetness of the Master of St. Mark. The author of the *Annunciation* appears influenced by Filippo Lippi. As for the Master of the Nativity of cell five, one may well wonder if he was not the head of the enterprise, working for Fra Angelico just as Jules Romains did later for Raphael, for the whole of his work appears impregnated with the Gothic spirit which will eventually dominate in this artist when he is no longer submitted to the *frate's* influence.

The *sportelli* of the Annunziata, in which the influence of Fra Angelico becomes more and more remote, lead us quite naturally from the notion of an " atelier " to that of a school. The Museums of Italy, Europe, and America contain numerous pictures in which one recognizes the master's manner more or less weakened. One has the impression that after Fra Angelico's death, his " atelier " continued to produce pious images inspired by his works for the benefit of a religious clientèle. The style of the predella in particular seems to have had much success and to have prolonged itself for a long time. Many of these little works, some of which are rather coarse in execution cause the art of Fra Angelico to regress towards a primitiveness which, although not devoid of charm, remains nevertheless very foreign to his profound spirit (Pl. 180). These artists accomplish moreover the liaison with the narrator painters of the *cassoni*, on whom Fra Angelico exerted indirectly a very perceptible influence.

Thus, like Giotto, Raphael, or the foreman of a Cathedral portal in the Middle-Ages, Fra Angelico should be considered as a sort of master-workman directing the gestures of numerous subordinates. Thanks to his gifts of sympathy and of love, he succeeded in communicating to his assistants something of the mystic ardour of his soul. All that was more or less connected with him partook of the prestige of his art. But in that abundant ensemble a few rarer works have received the unique impress of genius.

BIOGRAPHICAL NOTES

Luca SIGNORELLI
Portrait of Fra Angelico. Fresco from the Last Judgment.
Orvieto Cathedral.

1387. Birth of Guido or Guidolino di Pietro, near the village of Viccio, in the Province of Mugello.

1407. Carried away by the preaching of Fra Giovanni Dominici, Guido di Pietro and his younger brother Benedetto enter the Convent of St. Dominic at Fiesole which sheltered the Order of the Observance, founded by that disciple of St. Catherine of Siena who wished to restore to the dominican order the purity of its primitive rule and whose apostolate was a tentative reaction against the growing humanist spirit. The two brothers went to the Convent of Cortona to undergo their noviciate. It was there that Guido took the name of Fra Giovanni.

1408. The two novices return to Fiesole.

1409. The monks of Fiesole, who support pope Gregory XII against Alexander V, recognized by the City of Florence as the General of the Order are obliged to seek refuge in the Convents of Foligno and of Cortona.

1414. The whole community settles in Cortona.

1418. The Council of Constance having put an end to the schism, the brothers return to their Fiesole convent.

1432. Execution of an *Annunciation* (now lost) for the Convent of San Alessandro, at Brescia.

1433. July 11th. The Florentine corporation of the Linaiuoli, (flax merchants) orders a large retable in the shape of a tabernacle which is to-day in the Museum of St. Mark.

1435. On the instigation of Eugenius IV, a part of the community of Fiesole is transferred to San Giorgio Olt'Arno, the Convent of the Sylvestrians, in Florence.

1436-1443. The Convent of St. Mark attributed to the Dominicans of the Observance, is rebuilt by Michelozzo at the expense of Cosimo de' Medici. Fra Angelico decorates it with frescoes.

1437. Execution of the retable of St. Dominic at Perugia. (Vanucci Gallery, Perugia).

1438. Domenico Veneziano, writing to Pietro de' Medici to ask him to recommend him to Cosimo in view of obtaining an order for a picture, mentions Fra Giovanni and Fra Filippo Lippi as great painters of Florence having already produced an important work.

1441. Consecration of the Church of the Convent of St. Mark.

1442. Consecration of the Convent of St. Mark on the day of the Epiphany, in the presence of Pope Eugenius IV.

1445. Pope Eugenius IV who must have known Fra Angelico during his exile in Florence, calls the latter to Rome to paint the frescoes (now destroyed) of the Chapel of the Holy Sacrament, of St. Peter's, Rome.

1447. May 14th. Fra Angelico " *tam egregius magister Pictor* ", passes a contract with the vestry of the Dome of Orvieto. According to it, he will be obliged to spend the three summer months of each year in this city until he shall have finished the work undertaken at the Vatican —, in order to paint a *Last Judgement* in the Chapel of San Brizio. The contract designs the artist as being " *famosus ultra alios pictores ytalicos* ".
Fra Giovanni passes indeed three months of the summer at Orvieto — from June to September 1447; but he will make no other sojourn there. He begins the decoration of the Chapel of San Brizio which he will leave unfinished, and which will later be completed by Luca Signorelli. During the work, one of his assistants Giovanni d'Antonio, fell off from a scaffolding and killed himself. It is possible that Fra Angelico's sensitive soul was deeply struck by this unfortunate accident and that it prevented him from returning to Orvieto.

1447-1449. The Vatican records mention payments made to Fra Angelico and to his " atelier ". Six aids are alluded to in these accounts. The works to which these payments refer are not indicated. No doubt were they concerned with the frescoes of the Chapel of the Holy Sacrament rather than with those of the Chapel known as the " studio " of Nicholas V.

1443. Cosimo de' Medici orders round about this date four panels for the cupboard of the Treasure of the Santissima Annunziata (to-day preserved at the Museum of St. Mark).

1449. Resiliation of the contract passed between Fra Angelico and the vestry-board of the Dome of Orvieto. In the second part of this same year Fra Angelico returns to the Convent of Fiesole where he is elected Prior by his Brethren .

1452. Whilst in Fiesole, he refuses an order to decorate a Chapel of the Choir of the Prato Cathedral.

1454. Fra Angelico is proposed, together with Domenico Veneziano and Fra Filippo Lippi, to estimate the frescoes entrusted to Bonfigli in the Chapel of the Priors, of the Public Palace at Perugia.

1455. Death of Fra Angelico in Rome, on March 18th. He is buried in the Dominican convent of Santa Maria Sopra Minerva. It was no doubt during the stay which preceded his death that he painted the frescoes of the " studio " of Nicholas V.

BRIEF BIBLIOGRAPHY

ANCONA P. d'. — *Un Ignoto Collaboratore del B. A.* (Zanobi Strozzi). L'Arte, VIII. 1908, p. 101. — *La miniature fiorentina*, Florence, 1914.

BEISSEL S. — *Fra Giovanni Angelico*, Freiburg, i. B. 1895, 2nd ed. 1905; transl. into Fr. by J. Heilbig in Revue de l'Art Chrétien 1897-1898.

BERGAM. — *Beato Angelico*, M. L. Gemgaro, 1944.

BERKINS. — *La Descente de la Croix de Saint-Marc*, Albin Michel, Paris, undated.

BROUSSOLE. — *Fra Angelico*, Paris 1902. *La critique mystique et Fra Angelico*, Université Catholique, 1898.

CARTIER E. — *Vie de Fra Angelico da Fiesole*, Paris, 1902.

CIRAOLO C. e B. M. ARIB. — *Il Beato Angelico e le sue opere*, Bergamo, 1925.

CIUTI P.P. — *Beato Angelico*, Florence, 1940.

CLERISSAC Père. — *Fra Angelico et le Surnaturel*, Revue Thomiste, 1901.

COCHIN H.C. — *Le Bienheureux Fra Angelico da Fiesole*, Paris, 1906.

CRAWFORD V. — *Fra Angelico*, London, 1900.

CLARENSINI A.N.F. — *Les Fresques de Saint-Marc à Florence*, 1 vol. in-folio, 28 colour plates. Amilcaro Pitti, Milan, undated.

DOUGLAS Langton. — *Fra Angelico*, London, 1901.

FORSTER E. J. — *Leben und Werken der Fra Giovanni Angelico*, Rymsburg, 1859.

GOODWIN T. — *The Life of Fra Angelico*, London, 1861.

HAUSENSTEIN. — *Das Gastgeschenk*, Vienne-Munich, 1923. *Fra Angelico*, Munich, 1923.

MAIONE J. — *Fra Giovanni Dominici e Beato Angelico*, l'Arte, 1914, pp. 301, 381.

MARCHESE. — *Memorie dei piu insigni pittori... dominicani* I, Florence, 1854, p. 185.

MURATOFF. — *Fra Angelico*, Paris, undated.

NEWNESS. — *Fra Angelico*, London, 1906.

NIEUWBARN. — *Fra Angelico*, Leyden, 1901.

PAPINI B. — *Fra Giovanni Angelico*, Bologna, 1925.

PERATE A. et MARTY A. — *Les Fresques de Fra Angelico à San Marco*, Florence, Paris, 1914.

PICHON A. — *Fra Angelico*, Les Maîtres de l'Art, Paris, 1922.

PHILIMORE C. — *Fra Angelico*, London, 1881.

REGAMEY R.P. PIE. — Special number of " L'Art Sacré ", 8, (October 1946), *La valeur permanente et l'inactualité de Fra Angelico*.

ROTHES W. — *Die Darstellungen des Fra Giovanni Angelico aus den Leben Christi und Mariae*, Strasbourg, 1902.

SCHLEGEL W. von. — *Johan V. F.* Leipzig, 1846.

SCHNEIDER E. — *Fra Angelico*, Paris, 1926.

SCHNEIDER E. — *Fra Angelico*, 1938.

SCHOTTMULLER F. — *Fra Angelico (Klassiker der Kunst)*, Stuttgart-Berlin-Leipzig, 2nd ed. 1924; F. ed. Paris, 1911.

SINIBALDI Giulia. — *Il museo di Marco in Firenze*, Rome, 1936.

SORTAIT G. — *Fra Angelico et B. Gozzoli*, Lille, Paris, 1905.

STALEY E. — *Fra Angelico*, London.

STERLING M. — *Die Entwickelung der Komposition in den Werken des Fra Giovanni Angelico da Fiesole*, Zurich, 1919.

STRUNK J. — *Fra Angelico aus den Dominikanes Orden*, Muncher Gladbach, 1916.

SUPINO B. — *Beato Angelico*, Florence, 1901, in Thieme-Becker : " Kunstler Lexikon ", I, p. 516.

SWESSTER. — *Fra Angelico*, Boston, 1879.

TUMIATI D. — *Fra Angelico*, Florence, 1897.

VAN MARLE R. — *The Development of the Italian Schools of Painting*, Vol. X (1928), p. 52 (complete bibliography).

VASARI. — Minanesi edition, II, p. 125.

VILLAIN M. — *Fra Angelico*. Pélerinage entre Rome et Florence, Issoudun, 1932.

WILLIAMSON G. C. — *Fra Angelico*, London, 1901.

WURM A. — *Meister und Schularbeit in F.A.'s Werk*, Strasbourg, 1907.

ZUCCATO. — *Fra Angelico da Fiesole*, Vicenze, 1913.

HIC IACET VENE PICTOR FR IO DE FLO ORDIS PDICATO XLVII

NON MIHI SIT LAVDI QVOD ERAM VELVT ALTER APELLES
SED QVOD LVCRA TVIS OMNIA CHRISTE DABAM
ALTERA NAM TERRIS OPERA EXTANT ALTERA CAELO
VRBS ME IOANNEM FLOS TVLIT ETRVRIAE

M
CCCO
L
V

TOMBSTONE OF FRA ANGELICO
in the Church of Santa Maria Sopra Minerva, Rome. Photo Alinari.

EPITAPH OF FRA ANGELICO

on his tombstone
at Santa Maria Sopra Minerva in Rome.

Hic jacet vene. Pictor

Fra Jo. De Flor. ord. S. Pdicato 14 LV

M
C C C C
L
V

Non mihi sit laudi, quod eram velut alter Apelles
Sed quod lucra tuis omnia, Christe, dabam;
Altera nam terris opera extant, altera, cœlo;
Urbs me Johannem Flos tulit Etruriæ

———————

Here lies the venerable Painter
Brother John of Florence of the Order of the Predicant Brethren
1455

Do not glorify me for having been like another Apelles
But for having given to thine, Christ, the wages of my work.
For the gifts of the earth are different and different those of Heaven.
I, John, saw the light in the city which is the flower of Etruria.

SANTA MARIA NOVELLA
RELIQUARY

Museum of San Marco, Florence. Photo Hyperion.

LE RELIQUAIRE
DE SANTA MARIA NOVELLA

Musée de Saint-Marc, Florence. Photo Hypérion.

THE ANNUNCIATION
Santa Maria Novella Reliquary
Museum of San Marco, Florence. Photo Brogi.

L'ANNONCIATION
Reliquaire de Santa Maria Novella
Musée de Saint-Marc, Florence. Photo Brogi.

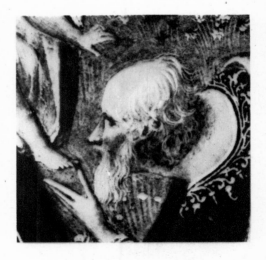

THE ADORATION OF THE MAGI
Santa Maria Novella Reliquary
Museum of San Marco, Florence. Photo Brogi.

L'ADORATION DES MAGES
Reliquaire de Santa Maria Novella
Musée de Saint-Marc, Florence. Photo Brogi.

THE VIRGIN OF THE STAR
Museum of San Marco, Florence. Photo Anderson.

LA VIERGE A L'ÉTOILE
Musée de Saint-Marc, Florence. Photo Anderson.

THE VIRGIN ENTHRONED
Vatican Gallery, Rome. Photo Anderson.

LA VIERGE TRONANT
Pinacothèque Vaticane, Rome. Photo Anderson.

THE VIRGIN AND CHILD
Museum of San Marco, Florence. Photo Alinari.

LA VIERGE ET L'ENFANT
Musée de Saint-Marc, Florence. Photo Alinari.

THE VIRGIN AND CHILD
Rijksmuseum, Amsterdam. Photo Rijksmuseum.

LA VIERGE ET L'ENFANT
Ryksmuseum, Amsterdam. Photo du Musée.

THE VIRGIN AND CHILD
(detail of pl. 57)
Vatican Gallery, Rome. Photo Anderson.

LA VIERGE ET L'ENFANT
(détail de la pl. 57)
Pinacothèque Vaticane, Rome. Photo Anderson.

THE CORONATION OF THE VIRGIN
(detail of pl. 64)
Museum of San Marco, Florence. Photo Hyperion.

LE COURONNEMENT DE LA VIERGE
(détail de la pl. 64)
Musée de Saint-Marc, Florence. Photo Hypérion.

THE VIRGIN AND CHILD (detail of pl. 58)
Museum of San Marco, Florence. Photo Anderson.

LA VIERGE ET L'ENFANT (détail de la pl. 58)
Musée de Saint-Marc, Florence. Photo Anderson.

THE VIRGIN AND CHILD (detail of pl. 59)
Rijksmuseum, Amsterdam. Photo Rijksmuseum.

LA VIERGE ET L'ENFANT (détail de la pl. 59)
Ryksmuseum, Amsterdam. Photo du Musée.

THE CORONATION OF THE VIRGIN   LE COURONNEMENT DE LA VIERGE
Museum of San Marco, Florence. Photo Anderson.   Musée de Saint-Marc, Florence. Photo Anderson.

THE DESCENT FROM THE CROSS (detail)
Museum of San Marco, Florence. Photo Alinari.

LE COURONNEMENT DE LA VIERGE (détail)
Musée de Saint-Marc, Florence. Photo Alinari.

THE CORONATION OF THE VIRGIN (detail)
Museum of San Marco, Florence. Photo Anderson.

LE COURONNEMENT DE LA VIERGE (détail)
Musée de Saint-Marc, Florence. Photo Anderson.

THE VIRGIN AND CHILD (detail of pl. 68)
Church of San Domenico, Cortona. Photo Alinari.

LA VIERGE ET L'ENFANT (détail de la pl. 68)
Église Saint-Dominique, Cortone. Photo Alinari.

67

THE VIRGIN WITH SAINTS. Polyptych
Church of San Domenico, Cortona. Photo Alinari.

LA VIERGE ET LES SAINTS. Polyptique
Église Saint-Dominique, Cortone Photo Alinari.

THE ANNUNCIATION
Church of Montecarlo di Val d'Arno. Photo Alinari.

L'ANNONCIATION
Église de Montecarlo di Val d'Arno. Photo Alinari.

THE ANNUNCIATION
Church of Gesù, Cortona. Photo Hyperion.

L'ANNONCIATION
Église du Gesù, Cortone. Photo Hypérion.

THE ANGEL OF THE ANNUNCIATION
(detail)
Church of Gesù, Cortona. Photo Alinari.

L'ANGE DE L'ANNONCIATION
(détail)
Église du Gesù, Cortone. Photo Alinari.

THE VIRGIN ANNUNCIATE (detail)
Church of Gesù. Cortona. Photo Alinari.

LA VIERGE ANNONCÉE (détail)
Église du Gesù. Cortone. Photo Alinari.

THE CORONATION OF THE VIRGIN   LE COURONNEMENT DE LA VIERGE
Musée du Louvre, Paris. Photo Musée du Louvre.   Musée du Louvre, Paris. Photo du Musée.

THE SAINTS AND ANGELS
OF THE CORONATION (detail)
Musée du Louvre, Paris. Photo Musée du Louvre.

LES SAINTS ET LES ANGES
DU COURONNEMENT (détail)
Musée du Louvre, Paris. Photo du Musée.

THE VIRGIN OF THE CORONATION (detail)
Musée du Louvre, Paris. Photo Musée du Louvre.

LA VIERGE DU COURONNEMENT (détail)
Musée du Louvre, Paris. Photo du Musée.

CHRIST CROWNING THE VIRGIN
(detail)
Musée du Louvre, Paris. Photo Musée du Louvre.

LE CHRIST COURONNANT LA VIERGE
(détail)
Musée du Louvre, Paris. Photo du Musée.

THE SAINTS OF THE CORONATION (detail)
Musée du Louvre, Paris. Photo Musée du Louvre.

LES SAINTS DU COURONNEMENT (détail)
Musée du Louvre, Paris. Photo du Musée.

THE SAINTS OF THE CORONATION (detail)
Musée du Louvre, Paris. Photo Hyperion.

LES SAINTES DU COURONNEMENT (détail)
Musée du Louvre, Paris. Photo Hypérion.

THE TABERNACLE OF THE LINAIUOLI
Museum of San Marco, Florence. Photo Brogi.

LE TABERNACLE DES LINAIUOLI
Musée de Saint-Marc, Florence. Photo Brogi.

THE MADONNA OF THE LINAIUOLI (detail)
Museum of San Marco, Florence. Photo Alinari.

LA MADONE DES LINAIUOLI (détail)
Musée de Saint-Marc, Florence. Photo Alinari.

ANGEL MUSICIANS (detail)
Museum of San Marco, Florence. Photo Anderson.

ANGES MUSICIENS (détail)
Musée de Saint-Marc, Florence. Photo Anderson.

80

ANGEL MUSICIANS (detail)
Museum of San Marco, Florence. Photo Anderson.

ANGES MUSICIENS (détail)
Musée de Saint-Marc, Florence. Photo Anderson.

THE VIRGIN WITH ANGELS (detail of pl. 84) LA VIERGE ET LES ANGES (détail de la pl. 84)
The Pinacotheca Vannucci, Perugia. Photo Alinari. Pinacothèque Vannucci, Pérouse. Photo Alinari.

TWO ANGELS (detail of pl. 84)
The Pinacotheca Vannucci, Perugia. Photo Anderson.

DEUX ANGES (détail de la pl. 84)
Pinacothèque Vannucci, Pérouse. Photo Anderson.

THE VIRGIN,
ANGELS AND SAINTS. Polyptych
The Pinacotheca Vannucci, Perugia. Photo Giraudon.

LA VIERGE ENTOURÉE D'ANGES
ET DE SAINTS. Polyptique
Pinacothèque Vannucci, Pérouse. Photo Giraudon.

THE VISITATION (School of Fra Angelico)
Prado Museum, Madrid.

LA VISITATION (École de Fra Angelico)
Musée du Prado, Madrid.

THE VISITATION
Church of Gesù, Cortona. Photo Hyperion.

LA VISITATION
Église du Gesù, Cortone. Photo Hypérion.

ST. DOMINIC AND ST. NICHOLAS
(detail of pl. 84)
The Pinacotheca Vannucci, Perugia. Photo Anderson.

SAINT DOMINIQUE ET SAINT NICOLAS
(détail de la pl. 84)
Pinacothèque Vannucci, Pérouse. Photo Anderson.

ST. DOMINIC (detail of pl. 84)
The Pinacotheca Vannucci, Perugia. Photo Anderson.

SAINT DOMINIQUE (détail de la pl. 84)
Pinacothèque Vannucci, Pérouse. Photo Anderson.

SANTA CONVERSAZIONE
Museum of San Marco, Florence. Photo Anderson.

LA SAINTE CONVERSATION
Musée de Saint-Marc, Florence. Photo Anderson.

THE DESCENT FROM THE CROSS
Museum of San Marco, Florence. Photo Brogi.

LA DÉPOSITION DE CROIX
Musée de Saint-Marc, Florence. Photo Brogi.

89

THE DESCENT FROM THE CROSS (detail)
Museum of San Marco, Florence. Photo Alinari.

LA DÉPOSITION DE CROIX (détail)
Musée de Saint-Marc, Florence. Photo Alinari.

THE DESCENT FROM THE CROSS (detail)   LA DÉPOSITION DE CROIX (détail)
Museum of San Marco, Florence. Photo Brogi.   Musée de Saint-Marc, Florence. Photo Brogi.

THE DESCENT FROM THE CROSS (detail)   LA DÉPOSITION DE CROIX (détail)
Museum of San Marco, Florence. Photo Alinari.   Musée de Saint-Marc, Florence. Photo Alinari.

THE DESCENT FROM THE CROSS (detail)
Museum of San Marco, Florence. Photo Hyperion.

LA DÉPOSITION DE CROIX (détail)
Musée de Saint-Marc, Florence. Photo Hypérion.

THE MARRIAGE OF THE VIRGIN
AND THE VISITATION
Church of Gesù, Cortona. Photo Alinari.

LE MARIAGE DE LA VIERGE
ET LA VISITATION
Église du Gesù, Cortone. Photo Alinari.

THE MARRIAGE OF THE VIRGIN
(School of Fra Angelico)
Prado Museum, Madrid.

LA MARIAGE DE LA VIERGE
(École de Fra Angelico)
Musée du Prado, Madrid.

THE VISITATION
AND THE ADORATION OF THE MAGI
Church of Gesù, Cortona. Photo Alinari.

LA VISITATION
ET L'ADORATION DES MAGES
Église du Gesù, Cortone. Photo Alinari.

THE ADORATION OF THE MAGI
(School of Fra Angelico)
Prado Museum, Madrid.

L'ADORATION DES MAGES
(École de Fra Angelico)
Musée du Prado, Madrid.

THE DREAM OF HONORIUS III
Musée du Louvre, Paris. Photo Musée du Louvre.

LE SONGE D'HONORIUS III
Musée du Louvre, Paris. Photo du Musée.

THE DREAM OF HONORIUS III
(School of Fra Angelico)
Church of Gesù, Cortona.

LE SONGE D'HONORIUS III
(École de Fra Angelico)
Église du Gesù, Cortone.

THE APPARITION
OF SS. PETER AND PAUL
Musée du Louvre, Paris. Photo Musée du Louvre.

L'APPARITION
DES SAINTS PIERRE ET PAUL
Musée du Louvre, Paris. Photo du Musée.

THE APPARITION OF SS. PETER
AND PAUL (School of Fra Angelico)
Church of Gesù, Cortona.

L'APPARITION DES SAINTS PIERRE
ET PAUL (École de Fra Angelico)
Église du Gesù, Cortone.

THE MIRACLE
OF THE INCOMBUSTIBLE BOOK. Predella
Musée du Louvre, Paris. Photo Musée du Louvre.

LE MIRACLE
DU LIVRET INCOMBUSTIBLE. Prédelle
Musée du Louvre, Paris. Photo du Musée.

THE MIRACLE
OF THE INCOMBUSTIBLE BOOK
(School of Fra Angelico)
Church of Gesù, Cortona.

LE MIRACLE
DU LIVRET INCOMBUSTIBLE
(École de Fra Angelico)
Église du Gesù, Cortone.

THE ANGELS' KITCHEN. Predella
Musée du Louvre, Paris. Photo Musée du Louvre.

LA CUISINE DES ANGES. Prédelle
Musée du Louvre, Paris. Photo du Musée.

THE RESURRECTION
OF THE YOUNG ORSINI
(School of Fra Angelico)
Church of Gesù, Cortona.

LA RÉSURRECTION
DU JEUNE ORSINI
(École de Fra Angelico)
Église du Gesù, Cortone.

ST. DOMINIC (enlarged detail of pl. 101)
Musée du Louvre, Paris. Photo Musée du Louvre.

SAINT DOMINIQUE (détail agrandi de la pl. 101)
Musée du Louvre, Paris. Photo du Musée.

ST. DOMINIC
RAISING NAPOLEONE ORSINI
Musée du Louvre, Paris. Photo Hyperion.

SAINT DOMINIQUE
RESSUSCITE NAPOLÉONE ORSINI
Musée du Louvre, Paris. Photo Hypérion.

THE MIRACLE
OF THE INCOMBUSTIBLE BOOK
(enlarged detail of pl. 98)
Musée du Louvre, Paris. Photo Musée du Louvre.

LE MIRACLE
DU LIVRET INCOMBUSTIBLE
(détail agrandi de la pl. 98)
Musée du Louvre, Paris. Photo du Musée.

AN ANGEL
UN ANGE
Musée du Louvre, Paris.

ST. DOMINIC
RAISING NAPOLÉONE ORSINI
(enlarged detail of pl. 101)
Musée du Louvre, Paris. Photo Musée du Louvre.

SAINT DOMINIQUE
RESSUSCITE NAPOLÉONE ORSINI
(détail agrandi de la pl. 101)
Musée du Louvre, Paris. Photo du Musée.

AN ANGEL (detail of pl. 99)
UN ANGE (détail de la pl. 99)
Musée du Louvre, Paris.

ST. THOMAS AQUINAS
Convent of San Marco, Florence. Photo Anderson.

SAINT THOMAS D'AQUIN
Couvent de Saint-Marc, Florence. Photo Anderson.

ST. PETER MARTYR
Convent of San Marco, Florence. Photo Anderson.

SAINT PIERRE MARTYR
Couvent de Saint-Marc, Florence. Photo Anderson.

THE MAN OF SORROW
Convent of San Marco, Florence. Photo Alinari

L'HOMME DE DOULEUR
Couvent de Saint-Marc, Florence. Photo Alinari.

CHRIST AS PILGRIM WELCOMED
BY TWO DOMINICANS
Convent of San Marco, Florence. Photo Anderson.

LE CHRIST PÈLERIN
ACCUEILLI PAR DEUX DOMINICAINS
Couvent de Saint-Marc, Florence. Photo Anderson.

ST. DOMINIC AT THE FOOT OF THE CROSS
Convent of San Marco, Florence. Photo Anderson.

SAINT DOMINIQUE AU PIED DE LA CROIX
Couvent de Saint-Marc, Florence. Photo Anderson.

SANTA CONVERSAZIONE
Convent of San Marco, Florence. Photo Hyperion.

LA SAINTE CONVERSATION
Couvent de Saint-Marc, Florence. Photo Hypérion.

THE HEAD OF CHRIST (detail of pl. 108)   LE CHRIST (détail de la pl. 108)
Convent of San Marco, Florence. Photo Alinari.   Couvent de Saint-Marc, Florence. Photo Alinari.

THE PILGRIM CHRIST (detail of pl. 107)   LE CHRIST PÈLERIN (détail de la pl. 107)
Convent of San Marco, Florence. Photo Anderson.   Couvent de Saint-Marc, Florence. Photo Anderson.

THE PRESENTATION IN THE TEMPLE
Convent of San Marco, Florence. Photo Anderson.

LA PRÉSENTATION AU TEMPLE
Couvent de Saint-Marc, Florence. Photo Anderson.

THE VIRGIN AND CHILD (detail of pl. 109)
Convent of San Marco, Florence. Photo Anderson.

LA VIERGE ET L'ENFANT (détail de la pl. 109)
Couvent de Saint-Marc, Florence. Photo Anderson.

THE VIRGIN (detail)
Convent of San Marco, Florence. Photo Alinari.

LA VIERGE (détail)
Couvent de Saint-Marc, Florence. Photo Alinari.

THE INFANT JESUS (detail)
Convent of San Marco, Florence. Photo Alinari.

L'ENFANT JÉSUS (détail)
Couvent de Saint-Marc, Florence. Photo Alinari.

THE TRANSFIGURATION
Convent of San Marco, Florence. Photo Anderson.

LA TRANSFIGURATION
Couvent de Saint-Marc, Florence. Photo Anderson.

CHRIST MOCKED
Convent of San Marco, Florence. Photo Hyperion.

LE CHRIST AUX OUTRAGES
Couvent de Saint-Marc, Florence. Photo Hypérion.

THE TRANSFIGURATION (detail)
Convent of San Marco, Florence. Photo Anderson.

LA TRANSFIGURATION (détail)
Couvent de Saint-Marc, Florence. Photo Anderson.

CHRIST MOCKED (detail)
Convent of San Marco, Florence. Photo Alinari.

LE CHRIST AUX OUTRAGES (détail)
Couvent de Saint-Marc, Florence. Photo Alinari.

THE ANNUNCIATION
Convent of San Marco, Florence. Photo Anderson.

L'ANNONCIATION
Couvent de Saint-Marc, Florence. Photo Anderson.

ST. DOMINIC (detail of pl. 117)
Convent of San Marco, Florence. Photo Anderson.

SAINT DOMINIQUE (détail de la pl. 117)
Couvent de Saint-Marc, Florence. Photo Anderson.

THE ANGEL OF THE ANNUNCIATION
(detail)
Convent of San Marco, Florence. Photo Alinari.

L'ANGE DE L'ANNONCIATION
(détail)
Convent de Saint-Marc, Florence. Photo Alinari.

THE VIRGIN ANNUNCIATE (detail)
Convent of San Marco, Florence. Photo Alinari.

LA VIERGE ANNONCÉE (détail)
Couvent de Saint-Marc, Florence. Photo Alinari.

THE CORONATION OF THE VIRGIN   LE COURONNEMENT DE LA VIERGE (détail)
Convent of San Marco, Florence. Photo Alinari.   Couvent de Saint-Marc, Florence. Photo Alinari.

THE CRUCIFIXION. SAINTS IN ADORATION
(detail of pl. 126)
Convent of San Marco, Florence. Photo Hyperion.

LA CRUCIFIXION. SAINTS EN ADORATION
(détail de la pl. 126)
Couvent de Saint-Marc, Florence. Photo Hypérion.

THE CRUCIFIXION
Convent of San Marco, Florence. Photo Anderson.

LA CRUCIFIXION
Couvent de Saint-Marc, Florence. Photo Anderson.

ST. THOMAS AQUINAS
(detail of the Crucifixion)

SAINT THOMAS D'AQUIN
(détail de la Cruxifixion)

ST. DOMINIC AT THE FOOT OF THE CROSS

Convent of San Marco, Florence. Photo Anderson.

SAINT DOMINIQUE AU PIED DE LA CROIX

Couvent de Saint-Marc, Florence. Photo Anderson.

THE CRUCIFIXION. THE HOLY WOMEN
(detail)
Convent of San Marco, Florence. Photo Alinari.

LA CRUCIFIXION. LES SAINTES FEMMES
(détail)
Couvent de Saint-Marc, Florence. Photo Alinari.

THE CRUCIFIXION. GROUP OF SAINTS
(detail)
Convent of San Marco, Florence. Photo Brogi.

LA CRUCIFIXION. GROUPE DE SAINTS
(détail)
Couvent de Saint-Marc, Florence. Photo Brogi.

THE CRUCIFIXION. ST. MARK (detail)
Convent of San Marco, Florence. Photo Alinari.

LA CRUCIFIXION. SAINT MARC (détail)
Couvent de Saint-Marc, Florence. Photo Alinari.

THE CRUCIFIXION. ST. DOMINIC
(detail)
Convent of San Marco, Florence. Photo Anderson.

LA CRUCIFIXION. SAINT DOMINIQUE
(détail)
Couvent de Saint-Marc, Florence. Photo Anderson.

THE MARTYRDOM OF SS. COSMAS
AND DAMIAN AND THEIR BROTHERS
Landscape
Musée du Louvre, Paris. Photo Musée du Louvre.

LE MARTYRE DES SAINTS COSME ET
DAMIEN ET DE LEURS FRÈRES
Le Paysage
Musée du Louvre, Paris. Photo du Musée.

THE MARTYRDOM OF SS. COSMAS
AND DAMIAN AND THEIR BROTHERS
Musée du Louvre, Paris. Photo Hyperion.

LE MARTYRE DES SAINTS COSME
ET DAMIEN ET DE LEURS FRÈRES
Musée du Louvre, Paris, Photo Hypérion.

A MAGISTRATE (enlarged detail of pl. 133)
Musée du Louvre, Paris. Photo Musée du Louvre.

UN MAGISTRAT (détail agrandi de la pl. 133)
Musée du Louvre, Paris. Photo du Musée.

AN EXECUTIONER (detail of pl. 133)
Musée du Louvre, Paris. Photo Musée du Louvre.

UN BOURREAU (détail de la pl. 133)
Musée du Louvre, Paris. Photo du Musée.

SS. COSMAS AND DAMIAN
BEFORE THE JUDGE
Old Pinakothek, Munich. Photo Hanfstaengl.

LES SAINTS COSME ET DAMIEN
DEVANT LE JUGE
Ancienne Pinacothèque, Munich. Photo Hanfstaengl.

SS. COSMAS AND DAMIAN
BEFORE THE JUDGE (School of Fra Angelico)
Museum of San Marco, Florence.

LES SAINTS COSME ET DAMIEN
DEVANT LE JUGE (École de Fra Angelico)
Musée de Saint-Marc, Florence.

THE BURIAL
OF SS. COSMAS AND DAMIAN
Museum of San Marco, Florence. Photo Alinari.

L'ENSEVELISSEMENT
DES SAINTS COSME ET DAMIEN
Musée de Saint-Marc, Florence. Photo Alinari.

THE MARTYRDOM OF SS. COSMAS
AND DAMIAN (School of Fra Angelico)
Museum of San Marco, Florence.

MARTYRE DES SAINTS COSME ET DAMIEN
(École de Fra Angelico)
Musée de Saint-Marc, Florence.

SANTA CONVERSAZIONE
Museum of San Marco, Florence. Photo Brogi.

LA SAINTE CONVERSATION
Musée de Saint-Marc, Florence. Photo Brogi.

SANTA CONVERSAZIONE
Museum of San Marco, Florence. Photo Anderson.

LA SAINTE CONVERSATION
Musée de Saint-Marc, Florence. Photo Anderson.

THE ENTOMBMENT
Old Pinakothek, Munich. Photo Hanfstaengl.

LA MISE AU TOMBEAU
Ancienne Pinacothèque, Munich. Photo Hanfstaengl.

140

NOLI ME TANGERE (Studio of Fra Angelico)
Convent of San-Marco, Florence. Photo Hyperion.

NOLI ME TANGERE (Atelier de Fra Angelico)
Couvent de Saint-Marc, Florence. Photo Hypérion.

CHRIST AS JUDGE
Orvieto Cathedral, Chapel of San Brizio. Photo Anderson.

LE CHRIST DU JUGEMENT DERNIER
Dôme d'Orvieto, chapelle San Brizio. Photo Anderson.

THE LAST JUDGMENT
THE PROPHETS' CHOIR (detail)
Orvieto Cathedral, Chapel of San Brizio. Photo Anderson.

LE JUGEMENT DERNIER
LE CHŒUR DES PROPHÈTES (détail)
Dôme d'Orvieto, chapelle San Brizio. Photo Anderson.

THE EVANGELIST ST. JOHN   L'ÉVANGÉLISTE SAINT JEAN
Vatican Gallery, Rome. Photo Brogi.   Palais du Vatican, Rome. Photo Brogi.

THE EVANGELIST ST. LUKE   L'ÉVANGÉLISTE SAINT LUC
Vatican Gallery, Rome. Photo Brogi.   Palais du Vatican, Rome. Photo Brogi.

THE ORDINATION OF ST. LAWRENCE   SAINT LAURENT CONSACRÉ DIACRE
Vatican Gallery, Rome. Photo Anderson.   Palais du Vatican, Rome. Photo Anderson.

ST. LAWRENCE GIVING ALMS   SAINT LAURENT FAISANT L'AUMONE
Vatican Gallery, Rome. Photo Anderson.   Palais du Vatican, Rome. Photo Anderson.

POPE SIXTUS II ENTRUSTING St. LAWRENCE
WITH THE TREASURES OF THE CHURCH
(detail)
Vatican Gallery, Rome. Photo Anderson.

LE PAPE SIXTE II CONFIE A SAINT
LAURENT LES TRÉSORS DE L'ÉGLISE
(détail)
Palais du Vatican, Rome. Photo Anderson.

ZACCHARIAS WRITING THE NAME
OF ST. JOHN (Studio of Fra Angelico)
Museum of San Marco, Florence. Photo Hyperion.

ZACHARIE ÉCRIVANT LE NOM DE JEAN
(Atelier de Fra Angelico)
Musée de Saint-Marc, Florence. Photo Hypérion.

ST. STEPHEN PREACHING TO THE PEOPLE   SAINT ÉTIENNE PRÊCHANT AU PEUPLE
Vatican Gallery, Rome. Photo Anderson.   Palais du Vatican, Rome. Photo Anderson.

THE MARTYRDOM OF ST. LAWRENCE
Vatican Gallery, Rome. Photo Anderson.

LE MARTYRE DE SAINT LAURENT
Palais du Vatican, Rome. Photo Anderson.

ST. BONAVENTURA (detail of pl. 152)   SAINT BONAVENTURE (détail de la pl. 152)
Vatican Gallery, Rome. Photo Anderson.   Palais du Vatican, Rome. Photo Anderson.

THE PONTIFF (detail of pl. 153) LE GRAND PONTIFE (détail de la pl. 153)
Vatican Gallery, Rome. Photo Anderson. Palais du Vatican, Rome. Photo Anderson.

THREE DEACONS (detail of pl. 146)　　TROIS DIACRES (détail de la pl. 146)
Vatican Gallery, Rome. Photo Anderson.　　Palais du Vatican, Rome. Photo Anderson.

WOMAN AND CHILD (detail of pl. 147)

FEMME ET ENFANT (détail de la pl. 147)

THE RISEN CHRIST
(School of Fra Angelico). Miniature
Museum of San Marco, Florence. Photo Hyperion.

LE CHRIST RESSUSCITÉ
(École de Fra Angelico). Miniature
Musée de Saint-Marc, Florence. Photo Hypérion.

STUDIO OR SCHOOL PIECES

OEUVRES D'ATELIER OU D'ÉCOLE

THE LAST JUDGMENT
Museum of San Marco, Florence. Photo Anderson.

LE JUGEMENT DERNIER
Musée de Saint-Marc, Florence. Photo Anderson.

CIRCLE OF THE ELECT WITH ANGELS
(detail)
Museum of San Marco, Florence. Photo Alinari.

LA RONDE DES ANGES ET DES ÉLUS
(détail)
Musée de Saint-Marc, Florence. Photo Alinari.

THE LAST JUDGMENT
Kaiser-Friedrich Museum, Berlin. Photo Museum.

LE JUGEMENT DERNIER
Kaiser Friedrich Museum, Berlin. Photo du Musée

THE BLESSED AND THE DAMNED
Wings of the Altarpiece of the Last Judgment
Kaiser-Friedrich Museum, Berlin. Photo Museum.

LES ÉLUS ET LES RÉPROUVÉS
Volets du rétable du Jugement dernier
Kaiser Friedrich Museum, Berlin. Photo du Musée.

ST. PETER PREACHING
Museum of San Marco, Florence. Photo Anderson.

LA PRÉDICATION DE SAINT PIERRE
Musée de Saint-Marc, Florence. Photo Anderson.

THE MARTYRDOM OF ST. MARK
Museum of San Marco, Florence. Photo Hyperion.

LE MARTYRE DE SAINT MARC
Musée de Saint-Marc, Florence. Photo Hypérion.

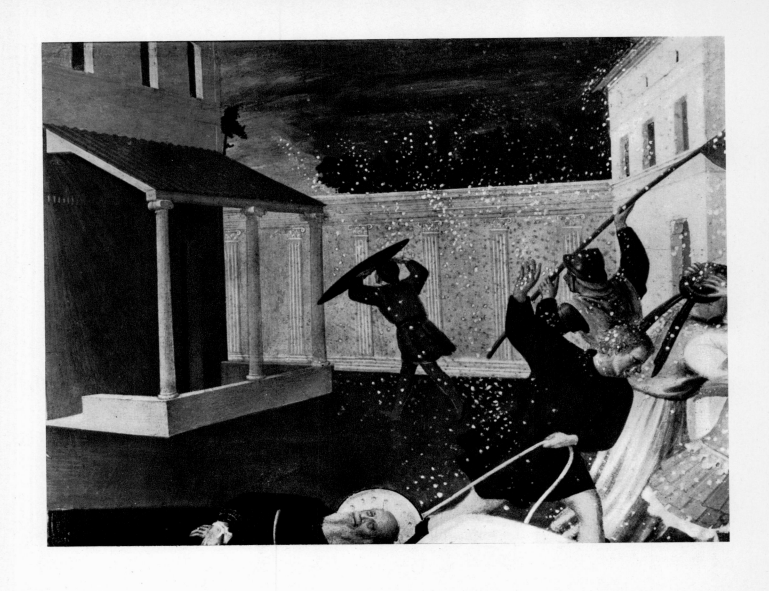

THE MARTYRDOM OF ST. MARK (detail)
Convent of San Marco, Florence. Photo Anderson.

LE MARTYRE DE SAINT MARC (détail)
Musée de Saint-Marc, Florence. Photo Anderson.

THE ANNUNCIATION
Prado Museum, Madrid. Photo Anderson.

L'ANNONCIATION
Musée du Prado, Madrid. Photo Anderson.

THE NATIVITY (Master of the Nativity)
Convent of San Marco, Florence. Photo Anderson.

LA NATIVITÉ (Maître de la Nativité)
Couvent de Saint-Marc, Florence. Photo Anderson.

THE ENTOMBMENT OF CHRIST
(Master of the Nativity)
Convent of San Marco, Florence. Photo Anderson.

L'ENSEVELISSEMENT DU CHRIST
(Maître de la Nativité)
Couvent de Saint-Marc, Florence. Photo Anderson.

THE AGONY IN THE GARDEN
(Master of the Nativity)
Convent of San-Marco, Florence. Photo Anderson.

LA PRIÈRE AU JARDIN DES OLIVIERS
(Maître de la Nativité)
Couvent de Saint-Marc, Florence. Photo Anderson.

THE DESCENT FROM THE CROSS
(Master of the Nativity)
Museum of San Marco, Florence. Photo Giraudon.

LA DÉPOSITION DE CROIX
(Maître de la Nativité)
Musée de Saint-Marc, Florence. Photo Giraudon.

THE VIRGIN (detail of pl. 117)
(Master of the Annunciation)

LA VIERGE (détail de la pl. 117)
(Maître de l'Annonciation)

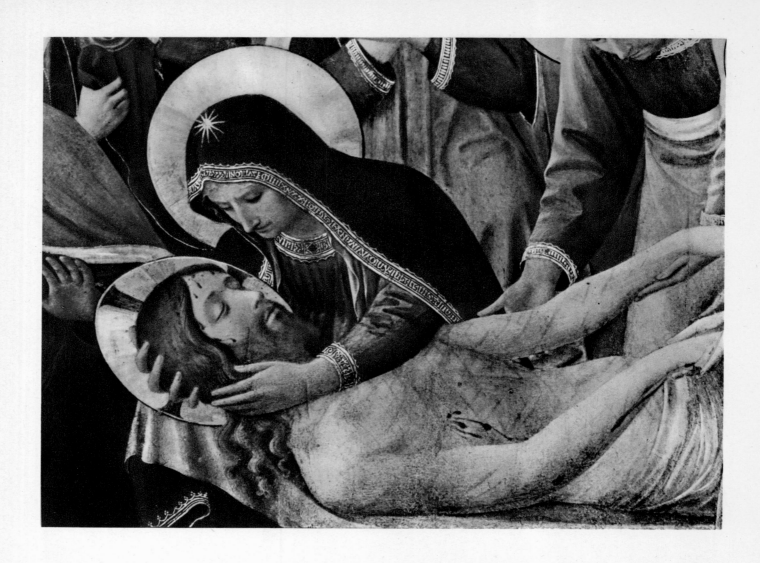

THE DESCENT FROM THE CROSS (details)   LA DÉPOSITION DE CROIX (détails)
(Master of the Nativity)   (Maître de la Nativité)
Musée of San-Marco, Florence. Photo Giraudon.   Musée de Saint-Marc, Florence. Photo Giraudon.

THE FLIGHT INTO EGYPT. Landscape (detail)
Museum of San Marco, Florence. Photo Hyperion.

LA FUITE EN ÉGYPTE. Le Paysage (détail)
Musée de Saint-Marc, Florence. Photo Hypérion.

THE ANNUNCIATION   L'ANNONCIATION
(Master of the Annunciation)   (Maître de l'Annonciation)
Convent of San Marco, Florence. Photo Anderson.   Couvent de Saint-Marc, Florence. Photo Anderson.

THE ADORATION OF THE MAGI
(Master of the Annunciation)
Convent of San Marco, Florence. Photo Anderson.

ADORATION DES MAGES
(Maître de l'Annonciation)
Couvent de Saint-Marc, Florence. Photo Anderson.

THE RESURRECTION
(Masters of the Nativity and of the Annunciation)
Convent of San Marco, Florence. Photo Alinari.

LA RÉSURRECTION
(Maîtres de la Nativité et de l'Annonciation)
Couvent de Saint-Marc, Florence. Photo Alinari.

THE FLIGHT INTO EGYPT
Museum of San Marco, Florence. Photo Anderson.

LA FUITE EN ÉGYPTE
Musée de Saint-Marc, Florence. Photo Anderson.

THE FLIGHT INTO EGYPT (detail)
Museum of San Marco, Florence. Photo Anderson.

LA FUITE EN ÉGYPTE (détail)
Musée de Saint-Marc, Florence. Photo Anderson.

CHRIST WASHING THE APOSTLES' FEET
Museum of San Marco, Florence. Photo Alinari.

LE LAVEMENT DES PIEDS
Musée de Saint-Marc, Florence. Photo Alinari.

THE PROCESSION OF THE MAGI   LE CORTÈGE DES ROIS MAGES
Strasbourg Museum. Photo Strasbourg Museum.   Musée de Strasbourg. Photo du Musée.

LIST OF PLATES

53. SANTA MARIA NOVELLA RELIQUARY. Panel, H. 33 in.
Museum of San Marco, Florence.
This work forms part of a series of four reliquaries from Santa Maria Novella, probably given by Giovanni Masi, Prior of that Convent, who died in 1430. Two of the reliquaries, the *Dormition of the Virgin* (Boston Museum) and the *Coronation of the Virgin* (Museum of San Marco, Florence) are rather poor studio pieces. Only the *Virgin of the Star* (pl. 56) and this work are by the master's hand.
A replica of the *Annunciation* is in the Friedsam Collection, New York, another one is in the Church of Saint-Louis-en-l'Isle, Paris.

54. THE ANNUNCIATION. Detail of plate 53.

55. THE ADORATION OF THE MAGI. Detail of plate 53.

56. THE VIRGIN OF THE STAR. Panel, H. 23 in. W. 20 in.
Museum of San Marco, Florence.
Part of the series of four reliquaries from Santa Maria Novella, together with the painting on plate 53. Considered by Alois Wurm to be the work of a pupil, this painting is in fact by Fra Angelico, but seems to have been somewhat spoiled by old restorations. The angels on the border are weaker than the central figure and must be by another hand.

57. THE VIRGIN ENTHRONED. Panel, H. 8 $\frac{1}{2}$ in. W. 6 $\frac{1}{2}$ in. Vatican Gallery, Rome.
The kneeling saints are St. Dominic and St. Catherine.

58. THE VIRGIN AND CHILD. Panel, H. 8 $\frac{1}{2}$ in. W. 6 $\frac{1}{2}$ in. Museum of San Marco, Florence.
The pose of the Virgin and Child is similar to that of the Virgin of the Monte Oliveto altarpiece by Don Lorenzo Monaco, now in the Uffizi.

59. THE VIRGIN AND CHILD. Panel, H. 29 in W. 20 $\frac{1}{3}$ in. Rijksmuseum, Amsterdam.
Formerly in the Oldenburg Museum. Exchanged in 1924 with the Rijksmuseum. This type of Madonna seated on a cushion is derived from the " Madonnas of Humility " frequently painted by the XIVth century Umbrian artist.
This work which we have placed side by side in the illustrations with the early Madonnas, should be contemporaneous with the frescoes of San Marco (ca. 1440).

60. THE VIRGIN AND CHILD. Detail of plate 57.

61. THE CORONATION OF THE VIRGIN. Detail of plate 64.

62. THE VIRGIN AND CHILD. Detail of plate 58.

63. THE VIRGIN AND CHILD. Detail of plate 59.

64. THE CORONATION OF THE VIRGIN. Panel, H. 44 in. W. 44 $\frac{3}{5}$ in. Museum of San Marco, Florence.
From the Santa Maria Nuova Hospital in Florence. This important work has sometimes been refused to Fra Angelico. Van Marle sees in it the collaboration of the master with Zanobi Strozzi. It may be queried whether the painting is a studio reduction after the Louvre masterpiece, or whether it is Fra Angelico's first idea. The quality of the painting inclines one to the latter hypothesis, in spite of some weak parts which oblige us to admit the intervention of a helper. The composition is on the other hand original, more spatial than that of the Louvre, which partakes of the monumental spirit of sculpture.

65. THE CORONATION OF THE VIRGIN. Detail of plate 64.

66. THE CORONATION OF THE VIRGIN. Detail of plate 64.

67. THE VIRGIN AND CHILD. Detail of the polyptych of plate 68.

68. Above : THE VIRGIN WITH SAINTS. Polyptych. Panel, H. 85 $\frac{3}{5}$ in. W. 94 $\frac{1}{2}$ in. Church of San Domenico, Cortona.
On the right St. Mark and St. Mary Magdalen. On the left, St. John the Baptist and St. John the Evangelist.

The predella of this painting, a studio piece, is but a simplified replica of the Louvre Coronation predella; it is at the Church of Gesù, Cortona (cf. plates 96 to 99). The saints, still very Gothic in spirit, are placed in a line on a plane and separated from the Virgin as in XIVth century polyptychs. The stiff style of their draperies is in contrast with the flowing robe of the Virgin. They seems to be the work of a pupil.
Below : THE ANNUNCIATION. Panel, H. 76 $\frac{3}{5}$ in. W. 62 in. Convent of Monte-Carlo di Val d'Arno.
Replica of the Church of Gesù *Annunciation* at Cortona. Muratoff considers this work as fairly weak. Fraulein Frieda Schottmuller and Van Marle believe it on the contrary to be by Fra Angelico. The great delicacy of execution to be seen in this little known painting makes me share the latter opinion. The artist merely sought to vary some of the colour effects and changed the scenery. The predella, inspired by the Cortona painting, is on the contrary a studio piece of the most mediocre kind. The building of the Monte-Carlo Church was finished in 1438, but according to tradition, this painting comes from the Church of San Francesco near San Miniato.

69. THE ANNUNCIATION. Panel, H. 63 in. W. 70 $\frac{3}{5}$ in. Church of Gesù, Cortona.
From the Church of San Domenico at Cortona. The number of replicas of this incomparable work bear witness to its celebrity. One of these is by the hand of Fra Angelico (Church of San Francesco at Monte-Carlo di Val d'Arno, plate 68 below). The painting from the Convent of San Domenico at Fiesole which is now at the Prado Museum, Madrid, and which was thought by Fraulein Frieda Schottmuller to be the original picture, is a somewhat fanciful variant executed in picturesque style, without the master's intervention, by a secondary painter thought by Van Marle to be Zanobi Strozzi (cf. plate 67 and predellas plates 84, 94, 95). The replica in the National Gallery is also the work of a pupil. A late replica in a different style is in the Church of San Martino at Mensola. The Cortona composition was taken up again in all its purity and under the direction of Fra Angelico at the Convent of San Marco (plate 174). It is known that in 1432 Fra Angelico painted an Annunciation for the Church of San Alessandro at Brescia. This work is lost. An Annunciation by a Venetian painter now in the Brescia church may be a reminiscence. Its composition is different from that of Cortona.

70. THE ANGEL OF THE ANNUNCIATION. Détail of plate 69.

71. THE VIRGIN OF THE ANNUNCIATION. Détail of plate 69.

72. THE CORONATION OF THE VIRGIN. Panel, H. 83 $\frac{1}{3}$ in. W. 157 $\frac{1}{2}$ in. Musée du Louvre, Paris.
From the Church of San Domenico, Fiesole. A major restoration made in 1939 has cleared this work of troublesome retouches and redeemed its true character. This restoration has shown to advantage the remarkable state of preservation of the picture, disfigured by old retouches which were far more extensive than the accidents they covered. Only one head has been severely damaged.
The predella will be found on plates 96 to 103. This and the predella of the Cortona *Annunciation* are the only predellas by Fra Angelico we possess of this period.

73. THE SAINTS AND ANGELS OF THE CORONATION. Detail of plate 72.

74. THE VIRGIN OF THE CORONATION. Detail of plate 72.

75. CHRIST CROWNING THE VIRGIN. Detail of plate 82.

76. THE SAINTS AND ANGELS OF THE CORONATION. Detail of plate 72.

77. THE SAINTS OF THE CORONATION. Detail of plate 72.

78. THE TABERNACLE OF THE LINAIUOLI. 1433.
Panel, H. 102 ⅓ in. W. 104 ⅔ in. Museum of
San Marco, Florence.
Ordered on July 11th, 1433 by the Linen Merchants'
Guild for the sum of 190 gold florins. Only the central
part is by Fra Angelico. Although the contract
specified that the interior as well as the exterior were
to be painted by the master himself, the wings and
the predella are studio pieces. The open wings show
St. John the Baptist and St. Mark, when closed,
St. Mark and St. Peter. The predella is by the same
hand as *Zaccharias writing the name of St. John*
(plate 149) and the *Marriage of the Virgin* in the
Museum of San Marco.
We know from a document that the wooden tabernacle into which the altarpiece was inserted had been
carved after a model by Lorenzo Ghiberti.

79. THE MADONNA OF THE LINAIUOLI. Detail of
plate 78.

80. ANGEL MUSICIANS. Detail of plate 78.

81. ANGEL MUSICIANS. Detail of plate 78.

82. THE VIRGIN AND CHILD. Detail of plate 84.

83. TWO ANGELS. Detail of plate 84.

84. Above : THE VIRGIN WITH ANGELS SURROUNDED
BY ST. DOMINIC, ST. NICHOLAS, ST. JOHN THE
BAPTIST AND ST. CATHERINE OF ALEXAN-
DRIA. 1437. Panel. Central part : H. 51 in. W. 30 in
Each side panel : H. 37 ⅓ in. W. 29 ⅓ in The
Pinacotheca Vannucci, Perugia.
Polyptych painted in 1437 for the Church of San
Domenico, Perugia. The right hand panel is the
work of a pupil.
Below : THE VISITATION (School of Fra Angelico).
Prado Museum, Madrid. Predella of the *Annunciation*
of plate 84 (below). Replica with variants of the
panel of plate 85.

85. THE VISITATION. Church of Gesù, Cortona.
Fragment of the predella of the *Annunciation* in the
same church (plate 69).

86. ST. DOMINIC AND ST. NICHOLAS. Panel, H. 37 ⅓ in.
W. 28 ⅔ in. The Pinacotheca Vannucci, Perugia.
Panel of the San Domenico of Perugia polyptych
(detail of plate 84).

87. ST. DOMINIC. Detail of plate 86.

88. SANTA CONVERSAZIONE. Panel, H. 60 ⅔ in·
W. 80 in.
Museum of San Marco, Florence.
From the Dominican cloister of Annalena, near Florence, to which it was given by Cosimo de' Medeci
in 1453. However it must have been painted earlier.
The presence of SS. Cosmas and Damian (left) proves
that the painting is due to the generosity of Cosimo
de' Medici. On the right : St. John the Evangelist,
St. Lawrence and St. Francis.
The picture is extremely worn and retouched, difficult
to appreciate in its present state. The limpness of
execution may be due to its condition.

89. THE DESCENT FROM THE CROSS. Panel,
H. 108 ½ in. W. 112 in. Museum of San Marco,
Florence.
Altar painting from the Sacristy of Santa Trinita, a
church for which Don Lorenzo Monaco was commis-
sioned to paint several important works It was begun
by the Camaldolite artist who painted only the three
pediments (see one of these at the end of this table).
Fra Angelico finished it several years later.
Kneeling in the foreground we see St. John Gualbert,
the founder of the Order of Vallombrosa to which
Santa Trinita belonged. According to Vasari the
man with a hood on the right is Michelozzo.
The collaboration of an assistant may be discerned
especially in the left hand group. This assistant,
one of those who worked on the frescoes in the Convent
of San Marco, is the author of the Nativity in Cell 5.
The picture was restored somewhat indiscreetly in 1841

90. THE DESCENT FROM THE CROSS. Detail of plate 89.

91. THE DESCENT FROM THE CROSS. Detail of plate 89.

92. THE DESCENT FROM THE CROSS. Detail of plate 89.

93. THE DESCENT FROM THE CROSS. Detail of plate 89.

94. Above : THE MARRIAGE OF THE VIRGIN AND
THE VISITATION. Church of Gesù, Cortona.

Two scenes from the predella of the Gesù *Annunciation* (plate 69). This predella depicts six episodes
from the life of the Virgin. The first four are among
the most beautiful works by the hand of Fra Angelico.
The last two (*The Presentation in the Temple and
The Death of the Virgin*) are the work of a pupil.
Studio replicas of this predella are to be seen under
the Prado and the Monte-Carlo di Val d'Arno Annunciations.
Below : THE MARRIAGE OF THE VIRGIN (School
of Fra Angelico). Prado Museum, Madrid, predella
panel from the *Annunciation* on plate 176.

95. Above : THE VISITATION AND THE ADORATION
OF THE MAGI. Church of Gesù, Cortone.
Part of the same predella as plate 94.
Below : THE ADORATION OF THE MAGI (School
of Fra Angelico). Prado Museum, Madrid. Predella
panel from the *Annunciation* reproduced on plate 167.
Replica with variants of the predella panel from the
Church of Gesù at Cortona.

96. THE DREAM OF HONORIUS III.
Above : predella of the *Coronation of the Virgin*,
Musée du Louvre, Paris.
Below : studio replica, Church of Gesù, Cortona.
The *Coronation of the Virgin* predella at the Louvre
relates several episodes from the life of St. Dominic.
It is unquestionably the finest of the three predellas
painted by Fra Angelico himself.
An important restoration made in 1939 cleared the
work from numerous retouches and revealed its
true freshness. It had, moreover, been but slightly
affected by time, except as regards the central panel
(Christ rising from His tomb) which was greatly worn,
doubtless by the kisses of the worshippers. The
predella of the Madonna from San Domenico, Cortona
(plate 68) is now at the Church of Gesù. It is a studio
replica of the *Coronation* predella.

97. SS. PETER AND PAUL APPEARING TO ST. DOMI-
NIC.
Above : predella of the Louvre *Coronation of the Virgin*.
According to Van Marle, the colonnade of the Church
was probably inspired by that of the Hospital of the
Innocents, begun by Brunelleschi in 1421.
Below : studio replica. Church of Gesù, Cortona.

98. THE MIRACLE OF THE INCOMBUSTIBLE BOOK.
Above : predella from the Louvre *Coronation of the
Virgin*.
Below : Studio replica, Church of Gesù, Cortona.

99. THE ANGELS' KITCHEN.
Above : predella from the Louvre *Coronation of the
Virgin*.
Below : *The Resurrection of Napoleone Orsini*, studio
replica of the picture reproduced on plate 101. Church
of Gesù, Cortona.

100. ST. DOMINIC. Enlarged detail of plate 101.
(Macrophotograph of the Louvre Laboratory).

101. ST. DOMINIC RAISING NAPOLEONE ORSINI.
Musée du Louvre, Paris. Predella from the *Life of
St. Dominic* (see plate 96).

102. Above : THE MIRACLE OF THE INCOMBUSTIBLE
BOOK. Enlarged detail of plate 98. (Macrophotograph taken by the Louvre Laboratory of two
heads situated in the middle distance on the left
inside).
Below : ANGEL ADORING. Detail. Musée du
Louvre, Paris.
Although some authors contest it, this pretty little
piece seems to be worthy of the master's hand. However it may be by the " Master of the Annunciation ",
Fra Angelico's best pupil.

103. ST. DOMINIC RAISING NAPOLEONE ORSINI.
Above : enlarged detail of plate 101. (Macrophoto-
graph, Louvre Laboratory).
Enlargement of two heads of onlookers in the middle
distance on the left.
Below : THE ANGELS' KITCHEN. An Angel.
Enlarged detail of plate 99. (Macrophotograph,
Louvre Laboratory).

104. ST. THOMAS AQUINAS. Convent of San Marco,
Florence. Lunette, cloister of San Antonino.

105. ST. PETER MARTYR. Convent of San Marco, Florence.
Lunette, cloister of San Antonino.

106. THE MAN OF SORROW. Fresco. Convent of San Marco, Florence. Cloister of San Antonino, lunette over the refectory door.

107. CHRIST AS PILGRIM WELCOMED BY TWO DOMINICANS. Fresco. Fresco. Convent of San Marco, Florence. Lunette in the Cloister of San Antonino. This image of Charity is to be seen above the hostelry entrance.

108. ST. DOMINIC AT THE FOOT OF THE CROSS. Fresco, H. 135 in. W. 60 in. Convent of San Marco, Florence. Cloister of San Antonino. This fresco is placed near the church entrance.

109. SANTA CONVERSAZIONE. FRESCO, H. 80 in. W. 108 ½ in. Convent of San Marco, Florence. Fresco in the corridor on the first floor. The saints are not by Fra Angelico and may be attributed to an assistant, the " Master of the Nativity ".

110. THE HEAD OF CHRIST. Detail of plate 108.

111. THE PILGRIM CHRIST. Detail of plate 107.

112. THE PRESENTATION IN THE TEMPLE. Fresco, H. 59 in. W. 51 ½ in. Convent of San Marco, Florence (cell. 10). St. Peter Martyr and St. Catherine of Siena take part in the ceremony.

113. THE VIRGIN AND CHILD. Detail of plate 109.

114. THE VIRGIN. Detail of plate 109.

115. THE INFANT JESUS. Detail of plate 109.
    Document retouched by the photographers to conceal the cracks on the face.

116. THE TRANSFIGURATION. Fresco. H. 74 in. W. 23 in. Convent of San Marco, Florence (cell. 6). The collaboration of an assistant is apparent in the Apostles.

117. CHRIST MOCKED. Fresco. H. 76 ½ in. W. 62 ½ n., Convent of San Marco, Florence (cell. 7). The Virgin is by an assistant, the same who painted the Nativity in cell 5 and other frescoes.

118. THE TRANSFIGURATION. Detail of plate 116.

119. CHRIST MOCKED. Detail of plate 117.

120. THE ANNUNCIATION. Fresco. H. 73 ½ in. W. 65 ½ in. Convent of San Marco, Florence (cell. 3). There is a school replica in which the figures of the Annunciation in cell 3 have been placed in the scenery of the Cortona Annunciation. (Van Marle, op. cit. p. 177, fig. 98).

121. ST. DOMINIC. Detail of plate 117.

122. THE ANGEL OF THE ANNUNCIATION. Detail of plate 120.

123. THE VIRGIN ANNUNCIATE. Detail of plate 120.

124. THE CORONATION OF THE VIRGIN. Fresco. H. 74 in. W. 62 ½ in. The scene takes place in the presence of SS. Dominic, Benedict, Thomas Aquinas, Francis, Peter Martyr and Mark.
    The collaboration of an assistant, probably the " Master of the Nativity " may be discerned in the faces of the Saints.

125. THE CRUCIFIXION. SAINTS IN ADORATION. Detail of plate 126. Convent of San Marco, Florence.

126. THE CRUCIFIXION. Fresco. H. 18 ft. W. 8 ft. Convent of San Marco, Florence. Chapter House. The great Founders of monastic orders and Doctors of the Church are grouped around the crucified Christ on the right. On the left are those who assisted Christ on Calvary and SS. Cosmas, Damian, Lawrence and John. The collaboration of the " Master of the Nativity " is visible in the group of the Virgin and the Holy Women.
    The prophets of the arch and the Dominican saints of the lintel are mediocre studio pieces.
    Below : ST. THOMAS AQUINAS. Detail of the above.

127. ST. DOMINIC AT THE FOOT OF THE CROSS. Fresco H. 94 in. W. 68 in. Convent of San Marco, Florence. First floor corridor. The Saints seems to be due to the collaboration of an assistant, the one who painted the "Noli Me Tangere" of cell 1 and the Annunciation in the Corridor.

128. THE CRUCIFIXION. The Holy Women. Detail of plate 126.

129. THE CRUCIFIXION. Group of Saints. Detail of plate 126.

Kneeling from left to right in the foreground are SS. Francis, Bernard, John Gualbert, founder of the Vallombrosa Monastery near Fiesole, and Peter Martyr. In the middle distance, standing from left to right, are SS. Benedict, Romuald, founder of the Camaldolite Monastery between Arezzo and Florence, and Thomas Aquinas.

130. THE CRUCIFIXION. St. Mark. Detail of plate 126.

131. THE CRUCIFIXION. St. Dominic. Detail of plate 126.

132. THE MARTYRDOM OF SS. COSMAS AND DAMIAN AND THEIR BROTHERS. The Landscape. Detail of plate 133.

133. THE MARTYRDOM OF SS. COSMAS AND DAMIAN AND THEIR BROTHERS. Panel. H. 14 in. W. 18 in. Musée du Louvre, Paris. There are two predellas representing the life of SS. Cosmas and Damian in the style of Fra Angelico. One of these, nine panels of which are extant, dispersed between the Keller Collection, New York, the Alte Pinakothek, Munich, the National Gallery, Dublin, the Musée du Louvre and the Museum of San Marco, Florence (plates 132 to 137 and plate 140) is supposed to have been the predella of the high altar in the Church of the Convent of San Marco (pl. 138). However, the total length of the panels exceeds the width of the painting by over 70 inches. It may perhaps be thought that the panels were placed in two tiers, one above the other. But the altarpiece and the predella panels do not seem to be in the same style. The predella shows in its architecture the undoubted influence of the Roman period, which places it between 1445, the year of the departure for Rome, and 1450, the date on which Roger van der Weyden who imitated the central scene (The Entombment, plate 140) in his painting at the Uffizi, may have seen it during his Italian journey. The San Marco high-altar on the contrary shows no trace of the Roman style and seems to be somewhat prior to the predella attributed to it.
On account of the poor condition of some of these panels, their authorship has sometimes been disputed. Weisbach even goes the length of ascribing them to Pesellino. The quality of the Louvre panel which has reached us almost intact, bears witness to the master's personal intervention. The macrophotographs which the Museum Laboratory has made on my instructions vouch for the beauty of the work. The other predella is supposed to have ornamented the Madonna of San Vincenzo of Annalena (plate 139). The measurements do not contradict such a hypothesis; this sequence presents no analogy of composition with the former. Although Muratoff considers it to be an original work, these very mediocre panels bear no trace of the master's hand. Van Marle attributes them, for no particular reason, to Zanobi Strozzi.

134. A MAGISTRATE. Musée du Louvre, Paris. Detail of plate 133, enlarged by macrophotography (Louvre Laboratory).

135. AN EXECUTIONER. Musée du Louvre, Paris. Detail of plate 133.

136. SS. COSMAS AND DAMIAN BEFORE THE JUDGE.
    Above : Panel. H. 14 in. W. 18 in. Old Pinakothek, Munich.
    Below : School of Fra Angelico. Panel. H. 7 ½ in. Museum of San Marco, Florence.

137. THE BURIAL OF SS. COSMAS AND DAMIAN AND THEIR BROTHERS.
    Above : Panel. H. 14 ½ in. W. 17 ½ in. Museum of San Marco, Florence. (See note plate 133). An extremely damaged work, disfigured by many accidents and hideous retouches, but which by its balanced composition was one of the master's best.
    Below : School of Fra Angelico. THE MARTYRDOM OF SS. COSMAS AND DAMIAN AND THEIR BROTHERS. Panel. H. 7 ⅘ in. Museum of San Marco, Florence.

138. SANTA CONVERSAZIONE. Panel. H. 86 ½ in. W. 89 in. Museum of San Marco, Florence. Altarpiece from the high-altar of the San Marco Monastery church. On the right, SS. Lawrence, Paul and Mark; on the left, SS. Dominic, Francis and Peter Martyr. Kneeling in the foreground, the Medicean

saints, Cosmas and Damian. This work, which was probably one of the most important of the master's paintings, is unfortunately very badly damaged. It was conceived still in the spirit of the Florentine period; however the breadth of its composition heralds the Roman period to which it is probably very close. The architecture, of which but a moderate use is made, is still in the style of Michelozzo. It is possible moreover that it was put in place in 1440, the year in which Lorenzo di Niccolo's painting formerly ornamenting the high-altar of the Church of San Marco was taken down and given to the Church of San Domenico at Cortona.

139. SANTA CONVERSAZIONE. Panel. H. 67 in. W. 67 ½ in. Museum of San Marco, Florence.
Retable painted for the Franciscan cloister of Bosco di Frati, in Mugello, near the Villa of Caffagiolo belonging to Cosimo de' Medici who must have given this painting to the Brotherhood, as shown by the presence on the right, next to St. Peter Martyr, of the Medicean saints, Cosmas and Damian. On the left, SS. Antoninus, Zenobius and Francis. The style of the architecture enables us to place this retable in Fra Angelico's Roman period. Note the breadth of the niche in comparison with the painting on the preceding plate, which must be several years earlier. The niche here becomes a hemicycle which heralds that of the Belvedere of Bramante.
The collaboration of Benozzo Gozzoli, frequent during the Roman period may be discerned in this work.

140. THE ENTOMBMENT. Panel. H. 14 ½ in. W. 18 in. Old Pinakothek, Munich.
This panel, isolated by Frida Schottmuller in her book and placed by that author at another period of Fra Angelico's career than the SS. Cosmas and Damian predella, obviously formed part of the latter, as evidenced by the similar dimensions and the gilded Corinthian pilasters, the remains of the old framing, which may be seen on its edges as on those of the other panels. This Entombment must have been the center of the predella, as in the Louvre Coronation of the Virgin.
This composition inspired Roger van der Weyden in a painting probably done in Italy about 1450 and now in the Uffizi Gallery. The photographic interpretation of this work is not quite true and distorts its characteristics.

141. NOLI ME TANGERE (Studio of Fra Angelico). H. 69 ½ in. W. 54 ½ in. Fresco Convent of San Marco, Florence (cell. 1).

142. CHRIST AS JUDGE. Fresco. Detail. Orvieto Cathedral, Chapel of San Brizio.
During his stay in Rome, Fra Angelico went to spend the summer months at Orvieto, away from the pestilential heat of the Eternal City, and on June 14th, 1447 signed a contract with the vestry-board of the Cathedral for the decoration of the Chapel of San Brizio. He was to be assisted by several pupils, in particular Benozzo Gozzoli. One of these, Giovanni d'Antonio, was killed by falling off a scaffolding. Fra Angelico worked on this fresco only during the summer od 1447. He did not return to Orvieto and cancelled his contract in 1449. The decoration, left unfinished, was completed 50 years later by Signorelli who depicted himself standing beside the Dominican monk on one of the frescoes. (See fig. page 45).
The work is weakened by the indiscreet restoration it underwent in 1845.

143. THE LAST JUDGMENT. Detail from the Prophets' Choir. Fresco. Orvieto Cathedral, Chapel of San Brizio.

144. THE EVANGELIST ST. JOHN. Fresco. Vatican Palace, Rome. Vault of the Chapel known as the " Studio " of Nicholas V. Fra Angelico was called to Rome by Eugenius IV. The Vatican accounts show the presence of his workshop from March 3rd, 1447 to 1449. These accounts undoubtedly refer to the execution of the frescoes in the Chapel of the Holy Sacrament at St. Peter's in Rome, which was destroyed in the XVIth century. The frescoes of the Studio of Nicholas V must have been painted during a second sojourn in Rome, after Fra Angelico's term

as Prior of the Fiesole Monastery (1450-1453). The scene which represents St. Lawrence appearing before the prefect bears on the prefect's throne the date ADCCLIII which must be an alteration of MCCCCLIII committed during one of the numerous restorations borne by the whole fresco through the centuries. In fact the chapel underwent four restorations between 1572 and 1585, in 1712 and in 1815. The last restoration, made in 1925, freed the frescoes from the most obtrusive retouches. From an examination of the accounts, Muntz had gathered that the premises were intended to be the workroom, or studio, of Nicholas V. Recent opinions, harking back to tradition, maintain that it was rather a private oratory.

145. THE EVANGELIST ST. LUKE. Fresco. Vatican Palace, Rome. Vault in the Studio of Nicholas V. The Evangelists are generally considered to be school pieces, yet their grandeur is unquestionable.

146. THE ORDINATION OF ST. LAWRENCE. Fresco. Vatican Palace, Rome.

147. ST. LAWRENCE GIVING ALMS. Fresco. Vatican Palace, Rome.

148. POPE SIXTUS II ENTRUSTING ST. LAWRENCE WITH THE TREASURES OF THE CHURCH. Detail. Fresco, Vatican Palace, Rome.
The vista from the doorway shows a curious cortile of antique style recalling the porticoes discovered later at Pompeii, with columns directly bearing the roofing. This antique form must have established itself in Rome where Fra Angelico saw it.

149. ZACCHARIAS WRITING THE NAME OF ST. JOHN (Studio of Fra Angelico). Panel, H. 10 in. W. 9 ⅓ in Museum of San Marco, Florence. This may have been a panel from the predella of the Coronation in the Santa Maria Nuova Hospital (plate 61). It is close in manner to the predella of the Linaiuoli Tabernacle. Van Marle attributes it to Zanobi Strozzi.

150. ST. STEPHEN PREACHING TO THE PEOPLE. Fresco. Vatican Palace, Rome.

151. THE MARTYRDOM OF ST. LAWRENCE. Fresco. Vatican Palace, Rome.

152. ST. BONAVENTURA. Fresco. Vatican Palace, Rome.

153. ST. STEPHEN BEFORE THE PONTIFF. Fresco. Vatican Palace, Rome.

154. ST. BONAVENTURA. Detail of plate 152.

155. THE PONTIFF. Detail of plate 153.

156. Above : THREE DEACONS. Detail of plate 146. Fresco. Vatican Palace, Rome.
Below : Detail of plate 147.

157. THE RISEN CHRIST. School of Fra Angelico. Miniature from a choir-book. Library of the Convent of San Marco, Florence.

160. THE LAST JUDGMENT. Panel. H. 41 in. W. 82 ½ in. Museum of San Marco, Florence. From the Camaldolite cloister of Santa Maria degli Angeli.
The authorship of this very popular painting is now disputed by nearly all critics. Van Marle attributes it to Zanobi Strozzi. The extremely poetic conception of this highly mystical work is certainly due to the Fiesole master, but it was actually executed by pupils under his guidance. The circle of the elect and the angels in Paradise was inspired by a mystic poem, a laude by the Franciscan friar Jacopone da Todi :
Una ruota se fa in cielo
Dalli Santi in quel giardino...
Fra Angelico may also have remembered a homily chanted at the bedside of dying brothers in the Dominican monasteries. (See Louis Gillet : Histoire artistique des ordres mendiants, publ. by Laurens, p. 259). This composition was taken up several times by Fra Angelico's studio (The Last Judgment, Berlin, plate 162. Corsini Gallery, Rome. The Annunciata cupboard). It was famous in its day, as shown by the copies with a variant made by Giovanni di Paolo. A late replica of a rather doubtful nature changed hands at the sale of the Emile Gavet collection, June 1st, 1897.

161. CIRCLE OF THE ELECT WITH ANGELS. Detail of plate 160.

162. THE LAST JUDGMENT. Kaiser Friedrich Museum, Berlin.
   This work has been defaced and artificially transformed into a triptych. The copy made in 1567 by Bartolomaus Spranger for Pope Pius VII (Turin Gallery) shows that in its original form it was a single panel. The Corsini Gallery, Rome, has a reduction which is also a product of Fra Angelico's studio. The Ascension of the elect is the best part of the picture and the closest to the master's manner.
   The analogy between the figure of Christ and that of the *Last Judgment* in the Orvieto Cathedral suggests that this is a late work.

163. THE BLESSED AND THE DAMNED. Wing of the Last Judgment retable. Kaiser Friedrich Museum, Berlin.

164. ST. PETER PREACHING. Panel. H. 15 ⅓ in. W. 22 in. Museum of San Marco, Florence.
   Predella panel from the Tabernacle of the Linaiuoli. A mediocre late replica of this panel was in the Aynard collection, Lyons, sold on December 14th, 1913.

165. THE MARTYRDOM OF ST. MARK. Panel. H. 15 ⅓ in. W. 22 in. Museum of San Marco, Florence.
   Predella panel from the Tabernacle of the Linaiuoli *Zaccharias writing the Name of St. John* (plate 149). The identity of execution is undeniable. This artist may perhaps be one of the miniaturists of St. Mark. In the Marczell de Nemes collection (sold at Munich, June 16-19th 1931, cat. nº 10) there was a charming panel representing the Adoration of the Magi, somewhat analogous both to the Santa Maria Novella Reliquary and to the panel on the same subject in the Linaiuoli predella.

166. THE MARTYRDOM OF ST. MARK. Detail of plate 165. Museum of San Marco, Florence.

167. THE ANNUNCIATION. Prado Museum, Madrid.
   This painting was considered by Frl. Frida Schottmuller as an original work by Fra Angelico. However the execution is coarser and the inspiration more vulgar than those of the master. The work is a replica in picturesque style of the Cortona *Annunciation*; the pupil seems to have wished to correct and perfect the master's work. Van Marle attributes it to Zanobi Strozzi. Panels from the predella which was likewise inspired by that of Cortona are reproduced on plates 84, 94 and 95.

168. THE NATIVITY. Fresco. H. 54 in. W. 62 ⅓ in.
   The principal work of one of Fra Angelico's assistants whose style is deliberately archaic and whom I suggest calling, after this fresco, the " Master of the Nativity ".

169. THE ENTOMBMENT OF CHRIST. Fresco. H. 76 in. W. 63 ½ in. Convent of San Marco, Florence (cell 2). By the Master of the Nativity.

170. THE AGONY IN THE GARDEN. Fresco. H. 54 in. W. 61 ½ in. Convent of San Marco, Florence (cell 34).
   Although considered by Van Marle as an original work, it should be attributed to the Studio. It is by the painter of the Nativity in cell 5. The face of one of the Holy Women is identical with one in the Mourning of Christ, Museum of San Marco, by the same hand (plate 171).

171. Above : THE DESCENT FROM THE CROSS. Panel. H. 41 in. W. 64 ⅓ in. Museum of San Marco, Florence.
   From the Confraternity of Santa Maria della Croce, of a mortuary destination. This painting may with certainty be attributed to the Master of the Nativity. Below : THE VIRGIN. Detail from *Christ Mocked* (see plate 117). Fresco, cell 7. Convent of San Marco, Florence.
   This figure shows all the characteristics of the Master of the Nativity, while all the rest of the fresco is by Fra Angelico.

172. THE DESCENT FROM THE CROSS. Details of plate 171.

173. THE FLIGHT INTO EGYPT. Landscape. Detail of plate 177.

174. THE ANNUNCIATION. Fresco. H. 98 ⅓ in. W. 126 in. Convent of San Marci, Florence. First floor, corridor. Notwithstanding its beauty, most authors agree to withdraw this famous work from Fra Angelico. It is a simplified interpretation of the Cortona *Annunciation*, and the work of his best pupil, the author of *Noli me tangere* in cell 1 (plate 157). A school replica of this work, fairly weak, exists in a private collection (see Van Marle, Vol. X, fig. 98). It was a tradition of the Dominican order that an image of the Annunciation, which taught humility, should be accessible to all the brothers. This explains the presence of this painting in front of the stairway leading to the Dormitory in the Convent of San Marco. Below : The Angel.

175. THE ADORATION OF THE MAGI. Fresco. H. 70 ½ in. W. 141 ½ in. Convent of San Marco, Florence (cell. 39).
   This work which ornaments the cell of Cosimo de' Medici is by the same hand as the *Annunciation* of the corridor and the *Noli me tangere* of cell 1.
   It was probably destined to commemorate the consecration of the convent, which took place on the day of Epiphany 1442, in the presence of Eugenius IV who slept in this cell. It must therefore be subsequent to that date.
   Below : One of the Kings.

176. THE RESURRECTION. Fresco, cell 8. Convent of San Marco, Florence. The Resurrection seems to be the result of collaboration between the Master of the Nativity and the Master of the Annunciation. The angel, a truly beautiful piece of work, is by the latter.

177. THE FLIGHT INTO EGYPT. Museum of San Marco, Florence. This work, as well as that reproduced on plate 179, forms part of a whole consisting of 35 subjects divided into 4 panels which closed the treasure-chest probably ordered by Cosimo de' Medici for the Church of the Santissima Annunziata of which he became patron in 1448.
   This ensemble, which reproduces scenes from the New Testament preceded and followed by a symbolical panel, is a typical example of the parallel between the two Testaments which was one of the great iconographical themes of sacred art in the Middle Ages. As in the illustrations of the " Biblia Pauperum " of the XIIIth and XIVth centuries which pictorially express dogmatic truths for simple-minded folk, each panel shows above a text from the New Testament while the corresponding Old Testament text is inscribed below. The cycle is thus meant to be a real lesson in theology.
   One panel only, the one that bears the first six scenes from the Life of Christ, from the Annunciation to the Flight into Egypt, belongs directly to the art of Fra Angelico. It is probable that the painter's presence in Rome prevented him from undertaking this work personally. It must have been executed according to his instructions by some pupils who, left to themselves, often swerved from the master's style. That is why most of these paintings belong rather to what we have called the " school " of Fra Angelico than to his studio proper.
   Messrs. Berenson and Van Marle see in the *Flight into Egypt* the hand of Fra Angelico. I have shown in the text why, with M. Muratoff, I do not share their opinion.

178. THE FLIGHT INTO EGYPT. Detail of plate 177.

179. CHRIST WASHING THE APOSTLES' FEET. Museum of San Marco, Florence. Detail from the Annunziata treasure-chest. See note, plate 177. The scene takes place in the gallery of a rustic *cortile*, such as we have seen in one of the frescoes of the Life of St. Lawrence (plate 148). The Apostle standing with the pitcher is almost identical with one in a panel from the Life of SS. Cosmas and Damian.

180. THE PROCESSION OF THE MAGI. Strasbourg Museum.
   This charming little painting is an example of the " predella style " works in which the art of Fra Angelico joins northern picturesque traditions. Berenson attributes it to Domenico di Michelino. It seems to be by the same hand as a small Adoration of the Magi in the Vatican.